MONEY REVOLUTION

The Essential Fintech Handbook on AI Banking, Cryptocurrency, Robo-Advisory, Neo Banking, Crowdfunding, and More

Email: sergey@tsabolov.com

Website: www.tsabolov.com

LinkedIn: www.linkedin.com/in/tsabolov/

First published in 2024.

Paperback ISBN: 978-1-7383347-0-4
E-book ISBN: 978-1-7383347-1-1

Illustrations by Alexei Boiko

Please email me at sergey@tsabolov.com to let me know if you liked this book. This is invaluable to me – to hear from my readers! Please email me what you did not like and what you would change or add. I would love to hear your opinion. I want to base the next editions' corrections and updates on the readers' feedback. Thank you very much! I appreciate your help!

Sergey Tsabolov

THE MONEY REVOLUTION

The Essential Fintech Handbook on AI Banking, Cryptocurrency, Robo-Advisory, Neo Banking, Crowdfunding, and More

Sergey Tsabolov

Contents

Introduction

This book is an easy guide on how the world of money, banking, and finance is transformed by modern technology. All major areas of this transformation with the most disruptive forces in play are included in this book. These areas are AI banking, cryptocurrencies and blockchain, mass hyper-personalization, open banking, banking-as-a-service and embedded finance, neobanks, crowdfunding, insurtech, and robo-advising.

The book explains what kinds of startups are disrupting the industry, how many existing companies that have been successful for hundreds of years are suddenly facing the risk of extinction, and what kind of jobs disappear and emerge. Additionally, it describes how this transformation dramatically changes the daily lives of almost everyone, as most people use money and banking services every day.

You can read each chapter independently. Essentially, every chapter is an individual, easy-to-read story about a particular area of finance. Each chapter helps to clearly understand in which way this area is disrupted by modern technology.

The nine chapters included in this book are:

- AI bank of the future – transformation of banking with artificial intelligence
- cryptocurrencies, blockchain, and bitcoin
- mass hyper-personalization of financial services
- open banking
- banking-as-a-service and embedded finance
- neobanks – modern banks that focus on superior digital user experience
- crowdfunding and its key types
- insurtech – modern technologies that disrupt insurance
- robo-advising – automated money management tools.

Each chapter has a similar structure. They each explain the basics, cover how this area disrupts the world of finance, briefly cover all key concepts related to the area, list opportunities that arise, key challenges and issues, and offer a short quiz.

The book has been written to be an enjoyable read. It is meant to be as accessible and jargon-free as possible. It is very structured and includes examples and illustrations that help explain complex concepts in a very simple way. Additionally, the author uses simple language, considering that many readers are not native English speakers.

The book is a comprehensive, hands-on handbook on the future of money, banking, and finance. The book translates complex concepts into an easy, demystified guide. It helps one understand how the world of financial services will look in the near future.

CHAPTER I

AI Bank of the Future

"Honey, what has happened to our bank support? They are being so empathetic and humane! It looks like they are finally hiring the right people."

This chapter describes how AI (Artificial Intelligence) is transforming banking. The chapter covers what drives this AI transformation and the opportunities it brings. The chapter explains the key challenges faced in advancing AI tools in banking.

In this chapter

What AI Banks of the Future Will Look Like

Imagine taking your smartphone, calling your bank, and talking to a representative. She is available 24/7. She has almost infinite knowledge. She is never in a bad mood. She can customize her voice, manner of speech, language, and so on. Imagine getting only personalized, relevant offers that you need, efficient fraud prevention and cyber-security measures, easy identification and authorization, and low fees from the automated digital infrastructure. Imagine the bank that knows you better than you know yourself. This is the AI (Artificial Intelligence) bank of the future.

AI Bank: Basics

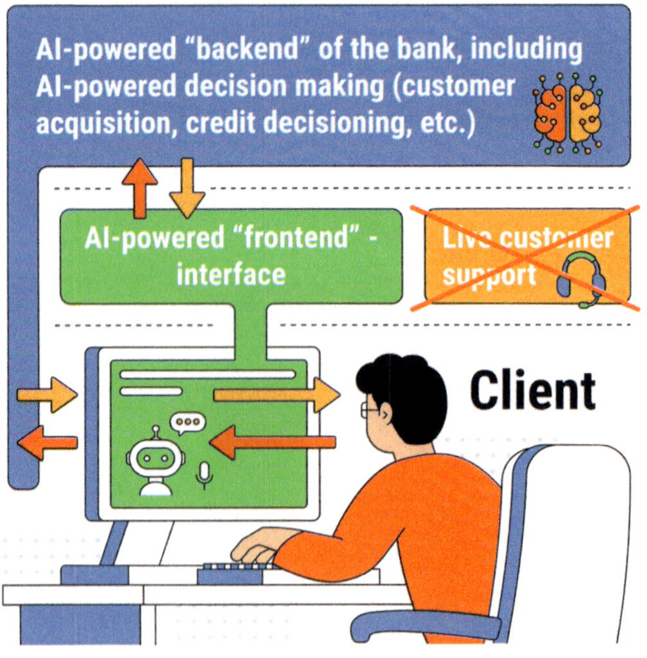

AI banking reinvents both back-end processes that are not directly visible to clients and front-end processes that shape customer experience. AI tools replace some human labor, legacy code, legacy processes, and infrastructure.

What Exactly is Changing

AI is profoundly changing the world of financial services. Banks are increasingly deploying AI-based tools to keep up with the competition. AI banking reinvents both back-end processes that are not directly visible to clients and front-end processes that directly shape the user experience. AI makes financial services more efficient, customer-centric, and secure. AI enables rapid innovation cycles across all areas and activities of financial institutions. Becoming "AI-first" for banks goes hand in hand with overall banking digitalization, including cloud computing, APIs (Application Programming Interfaces), and a focus on digital remote user experience. Becoming "AI-first" is the most transformative force.

AI Banking: Three Groups of Tools

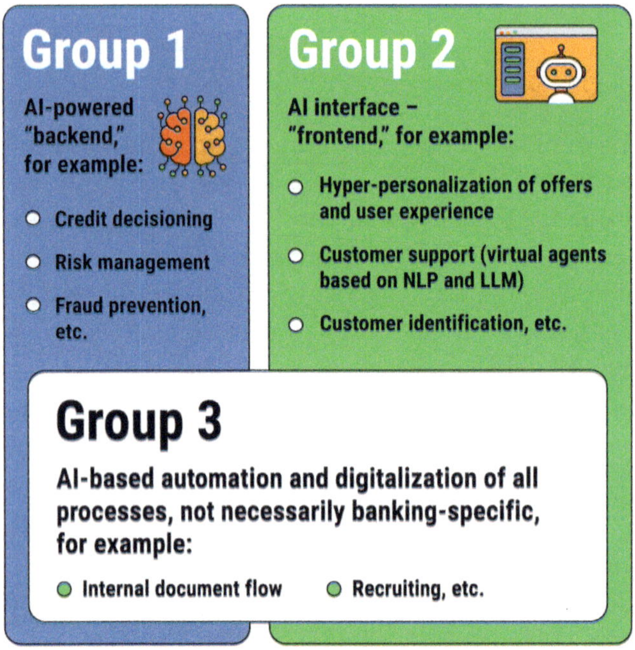

AI tools and technologies reshaping banking can be divided roughly into three groups: backend, frontend, and tools and technologies pertaining to both backend and frontend, not necessarily banking specific. The examples of Group 1 include credit decisioning, risk management, fraud prevention, etc. The examples for Group 2 include hyper-personalization of offers and user experience, customer support – virtual agents based on natural language processing (NLP) and large language models (LLM), customer identification, etc. The examples of Group 3 include internal document flow, recruiting, etc.

How Frontend is Changing

How would you communicate with perfect, live financial advisors if you could choose? You would probably ask them to talk to you and sometimes use visuals to illustrate certain ideas. Sometimes, you would also text. But the two most convenient forms of interaction for an average person are voice and images. A keyboard exists primarily because computers were not advanced enough to understand natural speech. This is what the AI bank of the future will do. It will talk to us and show us images.

Overall, AI changes financial services from the customer's perspective in several significant ways.

- Customer support will be available 24/7 and will be infinitely competent.
- Clients will be able to talk to voice and text virtual agents based on natural language processing (NLP) and customized large language models (LLM).
- Clients will enjoy a hyper-personalized and convenient user experience in the most convenient form, including voice and tailored visuals instead of lengthy texts.
- There will be an option to submit the information (documents, etc.) to the bank in any form because of the computer vision and optical character recognition (OCR) AI-powered tools.
- Offers will be hyper-personalized, delivered in real time, and based on the customer's goals, preferences, and situation.
- Services will be intelligent. Services will be based on a deep understanding of the client and will include forward-looking advice instead of just offering a short-term service. AI tools will help to understand customers deeply, including their emotions, by analysis of micro-expressions, voice tone, and so on. Also, this approach will be based on advanced predictive analytics that helps forecast the customers' behavior.
- Identification, authentication, and authorization will become easy based on biometric AI-enabled tools, including computer vision and facial recognition.
- Security measures will be enhanced.

- AI tools will allow rapid innovation cycles and create more agile organizations overall, able to change quickly according to customers' demands.
- Overall efficiency will increase, resulting in lower fees for clients.

How Backend is Changing

AI tools reinvent the backend of the bank. Deep learning-based advanced analytics, including predictive analytics, helps banks to better understand customer behavior and preferences. This increases efficiency and lowers the costs of many processes. For example, in fraud prevention and cybersecurity, deep learning techniques help detect fraud patterns and suspicious activities in real time. Similarly, many key banking processes are being reinvented, such as credit decisioning, underwriting and risk management, portfolio management, compliance, regulatory reporting, etc.

What Changes for a Customer

These are the primary areas being transformed by AI from the customers' perspective.

Hyper-Personalization

AI enables increasingly sophisticated and efficient tools to (1) gather abundant near real-time data, including big data about a customer or potential customer, (2) analyze this data, and (3) swiftly offer and deliver the service to meet the specific needs and preferences. This process forms the foundation of hyper-personalization. Hyper-personalization of financial services refers to the deep customization of services to meet individual or prospective customers' specific goals, situations, and preferences.

Robo-Everything

Robo-advisor is an automated, enabled by IT (Information Technology), investment advisory and money management tool. The concept of robo-advising isn't limited to just investment advisory and money management tools. We are gradually transitioning toward a "robo-everything" approach in the world of finance. This includes innovations like robo-mortgage advisors and robo-credit-score-building tools. Just as money management tasks are automated, other tasks, such as finding the best mortgage and deciding when to refinance or optimizing and improving one's credit score, will also become automated. We are moving toward "robo-everything" – a financial advisor who will take care of all our financial matters. This automated financial advisor will be able to open a checking account for you, advise on the best credit card, etc.

Different Approaches

Financial services companies deploy different approaches to reinvent themselves:

- in-house incubation
- investments in startups
- white-label solutions from other providers
- partnerships with technology companies.

How AI is Changing the Industry

AI tools are the most disruptive force in the entire financial services world. The AI-based approach in finance will become a standard. Competition will drive this approach to become ubiquitous. Financial institutions will have to adopt it to survive.

This brings a new level of service for customers. An approach based on AI will significantly enhance banking experiences for the customers and will democratize quality banking. An infinitely experienced and knowledgeable personal financial advisor will be available 24 hours a day, 7 days a week. Technology makes this possible for almost everyone.

As this approach reshapes the financial landscape, it presents significant opportunities for new startups entering the market. New players are more focused on technology than traditional players and can implement AI-based banking faster and better or build from scratch. Thus, they can compete successfully with traditional companies, attracting clients, particularly younger ones.

For incumbent banks capable of reinventing themselves, AI brings opportunities as well: efficiency, cost reduction, and better user experience. Traditional companies have their own advantages in competition with startups: reputation and existing clientele.

Big Tech (also known as Tech Giants) – companies like Google, Amazon, Apple, and Meta – might enter the banking area and provide their own banking solutions, potentially having a competitive advantage. Big Tech has unparalleled resources and expertise in AI technology, enabling them to deploy AI tools in various areas, including financial services. Aside from AI technology, these companies have customers, data, and access to capital.

Another group of companies can benefit from developing AI banking: providers of various AI tools and technological platforms that provide services and AI infrastructure to other players.

Potential Problems, Risks, and Challenges

For financial services companies, the challenge is to reinvent themselves completely and decisively to stay competitive. To survive, these companies must accept AI as a foundation and become AI-first. At the same time, they need to act with agility in situations of uncertainty: AI is a rapidly changing area. Therefore, the usual approach of slow traditional banks to "form a several-year strategy and then implement it" might be difficult. The strategy might need to be constantly adjusted on the fly.

AI technology can be viewed as one of the dangers for consumers because it gives a lot of opportunities for manipulation to banks and other financial institutions. With a deep understanding of a customer, including at an emotional level, and rich verbal and visual abilities, the banks will be able to persuade effectively. The banks' aim is to achieve profits, not offer optimal products to their customers. This means the banks are motivated to manipulate the customers using their full AI arsenal to persuade them to use products and services that customers do not need under conditions that are not optimal for them.

One of the possible solutions to this problem lies in the interaction of several AI agents. For example, the first one is the AI agent at the bank. The next is the customer's personal AI advisor. The bank offers a product or service. The advisor analyzes the offer and negotiates. The advisor focuses on getting objective information about your finances and the market. It objectively compares the offerings from many banks. Your advisor acts in your interest. There might even be a third AI agent – a regulator whose aim is to protect the customer.

Regulators will probably have to respond to the rapid development of AI capable of manipulation. This regulatory pressure may be challenging because it can be quite complex and difficult for genuine players to comply with.

Also, bias and fairness are two major potential challenges in this area. AI and machine learning models learn from existing data. If historical financial data has biases (for example, lower credit limits for certain groups of people), AI technology might perpetuate these biases, leading to unfair decisions.

Quiz

QUESTION 1.

How is AI (Artificial Intelligence) transforming the world of financial services?

A. AI introduces disintermediation.
B. Governments find it easier to control and regulate the financial services sector.
C. Customers benefit from superior products and services, with improvements ranging from user experience to personalization.

QUESTION 2.

How will AI change the way traditional banks work?

A. AI algorithms will help future banks achieve more efficient decision-making in customer acquisition, credit decisioning, investments, etc.
B. AI algorithms will help future banks create a better user experience by transforming the interaction between the user and the bank, including customer support.
C. Both A and B are correct.

QUESTION 3.

How is the user experience changing due to AI transformation of financial services?

A. The experience is becoming personalized to individual goals, preferences, and situations. Reactions are faster and in real time. There is improved clarity about banking information. Security measures are enhanced.

B. Interactions are becoming more convenient through voice responses rather than lengthy texts, and services become available around the clock.
C. Both A and B are correct.

QUESTION 4.

What opportunities does AI transformation present within the financial services sector?

A. It provides opportunities for older, traditional, conservative institutions with substantial legacy systems that resist rapid reinvention to solidify their position in the market.
B. It offers opportunities for new players, such as neobanks, to establish themselves in the financial landscape.
C. It allows finance professionals to rely on their "old" skills and experiences to become even more sought-after in the job market.

QUESTION 5.

What are the key challenges and problems for the further development of AI banking?

A. The potential for manipulation and biases.
B. Competition among banks (and other financial institutions).
C. Rising costs of banking due to increased hardware requirements driven by AI models.

Companies and Organizations to Follow

- OpenAI (https://www.openai.com) is a US AI organization and research laboratory offering disruptive AI tools. These tools are not specific to financial technology. However, they give some parts of the picture about how transformative these tools will be in all areas, including financial services.
- Neobanks: Many neobanks, in contrast to traditional banks, are much more agile and swift to implement disruptive AI tools.

People to Know and Follow

- Brett King is a renowned futurist and speaker who covers the future of business, finance, and banking. He is recognized as an influencer in financial services globally.
- Chris Skinner is one of the most influential people in financial technology in the United Kingdom and globally. He is an independent commentator on the financial services industry, financial technology, and modern digital banking.

Answers to Quiz

1. **Answer: C.** Option A raises the question of whether AI truly leads to disintermediation. Option B hints at the development of AI-enabled tools, simplifying regulatory tasks. However, option C most accurately captures one of the significant outcomes of AI in finance: enhanced products and services for customers.
2. **Answer: C.** Both A and B correctly describe the key ways AI is transforming and will transform banks.
3. **Answer: C.** The correct choice is C. Both options A and B accurately describe the major ways AI is revolutionizing the user experience in financial services.
4. **Answer: B.** The AI transformation is particularly advantageous for emerging entities like neobanks. While option A suggests benefits for traditional institutions, in reality, these institutions often face challenges adapting to a new AI-driven world. As for option C, while seasoned skills and experience are valuable, the evolving financial landscape also requires acquiring new skills.
5. **Answer: A.** Competition between banks (and other financial institutions) is a driver of this area, not a challenge. The AI approach does require substantial hardware resources, but this is not a major hurdle.

CHAPTER 2

Cryptocurrencies and Blockchain

"Honey, remember, after we invested all our money in bitcoins, we got a piece of paper with a strange mix of numbers and letters. In a row. Have you saved it just in case?"

This chapter explains what cryptocurrencies are. The chapter covers the basics of blockchain, modern cryptography, the concepts of DeFi (Decentralized Finance), tokens, fiat currency, NFT (Non-Fungible Tokens), and ICO (Initial Coin Offering). Also, this chapter explains how cryptocurrencies are changing the world of finance and what the challenges in this process are.

In this chapter

What Cryptocurrency and Blockchain Are

Cryptocurrencies are decentralized digital money based on blockchain and cryptography. Sometimes, cryptocurrencies are referred to as simply "crypto." Two technologies are the pillars of cryptocurrencies: blockchain and public-key cryptography. A blockchain is a system of immutable records of transactions in which the records are publicly available via a distributed database. Public-key cryptography refers to the system in which there are two related keys: a public key and a corresponding private key.

Example

Bitcoin is an example of a cryptocurrency and is the first cryptocurrency. Bitcoin is thought to have been born in 2008, when the first paper on Bitcoin was published. In 2009, Bitcoin's software was implemented as an open-source code. Satoshi Nakamoto, the father of Bitcoin, is considered to be a fictitious person. Satoshi Nakamoto is a pseudonym used by a person or group of people, who remain unknown.

How Blockchain Works

The above illustration explains how blockchain works. Alice, Bob, and Charlie each had 100 units of cryptocurrency. They can send this money to each other without any intermediaries, such as banks. The entire transaction history is public. Everyone (not only Alice, Bob, and Charlie) can see all balances and transactions. However, everyone does not see Alice, Bob, and Charlie's names. Instead, they are "represented" by public keys.

Blockchain

Blockchain is a system of immutable records of transactions in which the records are publicly available via a distributed database. Several things are important here. First of all, the records are immutable: nothing is ever deleted. Secondly, all these records are publicly available, not only to those who own currency.

Thirdly, there is no single copy of the database: it is distributed and can have multiple copies.

Everyone Can Have a Copy of Records

Everyone can have a copy of all records in the blockchain. This includes everyone – not only those whose information appears on the blockchain, like Alice, Bob, and Charlie. Daniel can have his copy just because he wants to. He does not need to explain why or ask anyone for permission. The records can be downloaded freely and analyzed extensively by anyone.

Basics of Cryptography: Two Keys

One of the technologies cryptocurrencies are based on is public-key cryptography (also known as asymmetric cryptography).

"Crypto" in the term "cryptocurrencies" refers to this technology. Public-key cryptography is a system based on two keys. Cryptographic algorithms generate a pair of related keys: a public key and a private key. The public key can be known to everyone, but the private key should be known only to the owner of the cryptocurrency. To use the currency – for example, to make a transfer – a private key is needed.

For example, if you have one bitcoin, you can manage your bitcoin only as long as you have your private key. If you lose your private key, your money is lost. If your private key is stolen, the thief can manage your money, for example, by transferring it to someone else.

Two Keys

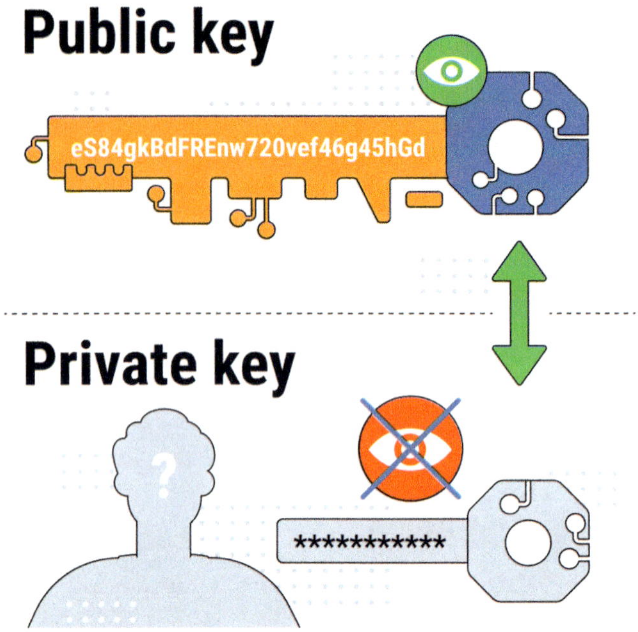

Cryptographic algorithms generate a pair of related keys: a public key and a private key. The public key can be known to everyone, but the private key should be known only to the owner of the cryptocurrency.

Various Cryptocurrencies

The second most popular cryptocurrency after Bitcoin is Ether. Aside from Bitcoin and Ether, there are many other cryptocurrencies. Sometimes, relatively less known and popular cryptocurrencies are collectively referred to as "altcoins" (alternative coins). There are various types of cryptocurrencies. Some cryptocurrencies have specific features that distinguish them from others. For example, there are "stablecoins." Traditionally, one of the key disadvantages of the cryptocurrencies was their unstable rate versus traditional (also known as "fiat") currencies versus other cryptocurrencies. This gave birth to "stablecoins" – cryptocurrencies whose rate is pegged to certain traditional currencies, for example, the US dollar.

Privacy, Anonymity, and Pseudonymity

Cryptocurrencies offer a key advantage: privacy. The transaction remains discreet when you make a payment or transfer money using cryptocurrencies. This is why cryptocurrencies, like Bitcoin, are often referred to as "electronic cash" or "electronic gold." When you transact with physical cash or gold, there's no clear record of the exchange, which enhances privacy compared to standard electronic payments. However, with cryptocurrencies, electronic records exist. These records show the transfer details between public keys but don't reveal the identities behind them. For example, in a Bitcoin transaction, while the public can see which public key sent an amount to another public key and when, the actual person behind that public key remains anonymous.

Cryptocurrencies can either be anonymous or pseudonymous. Anonymous cryptocurrencies operate entirely on the principle of concealing identities. On the other hand, pseudonymous cryptocurrencies, like Bitcoin, work on the idea that users operate under a visible pseudonym.

To illustrate, let us use an example. Suppose you own some bitcoins and are actively transacting – both sending and receiving funds. Throughout these transactions, you consistently use the same pair of keys: your private and public key. If, for any given transaction, it is somehow revealed that you are the owner of the private key, it immediately becomes apparent that you were behind all the previous transactions. This is because, in each of those transactions, you were identified by your pseudonym, which is your Bitcoin address.

Bitcoin address is a string of symbols that is derived from a public key. Public key is compressed and shortened to a public address.

What is Publicly Known and What is Not

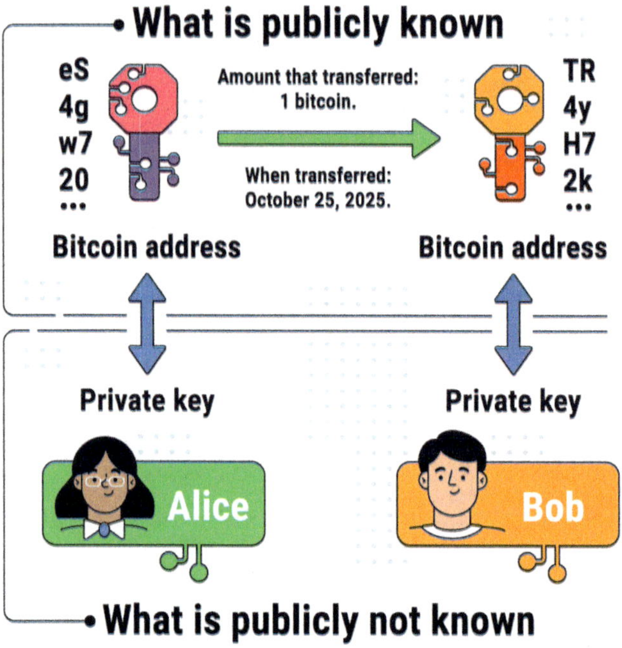

We can see the details of Bitcoin transactions on the Bitcoins' blockchain, which consists of publicly available records. These details are: how many bitcoins were transferred, when they were transferred, and from what Bitcoin address to what Bitcoin address. However, the identities of the individuals who own the bitcoins associated with these addresses remain undisclosed.

Crypto Exchanges

One of the major benefits praised by cryptocurrency enthusiasts is disintermediation. Essentially, there is no middleman dictating whether you can send or receive money. You do not need permission, nor do you have to navigate through processes like opening a bank account or verifying the source of your funds. However, the crypto economy does introduce certain intermediaries. Most notable of these intermediaries are cryptocurrency exchanges, often referred to as "crypto exchanges."

A crypto exchange is typically an online platform allowing users to buy, sell, or trade cryptocurrencies against other digital assets or traditional currencies. Many of these platforms also offer storage for your cryptocurrency. In such cases, some of the previously described aspects, like knowing your private key or the risk of losing it, become irrelevant. The platform acts as a middleman, managing the cryptocurrency on your behalf.

Interestingly, a growing number of retail banks, especially "neobanks," are beginning to offer similar services. Customers can now buy, sell, or trade cryptocurrencies and store them in a bank, just as they would with other assets, including conventional money.

DeFi (Decentralized Finance)

DeFi (Decentralized Finance) is a crypto economic concept of a financial system without traditional intermediaries. Such a system is built on the pillars of blockchain and cryptocurrencies. For example, in such a system, individuals can lend and borrow peer-to-peer without the traditional intermediary – a retail bank.

Tokens and NFTs (Non-Fungible Tokens)

The terms "token" and "tokenization" frequently come up within the realm of blockchain and cryptocurrencies. A token denotes a unit of value that's created on a blockchain. Essentially, a digital token (often just referred to as a "token") is a sequence of characters, including letters and numbers. Tokenization is the process of converting rights to an asset into a digital token on a blockchain.

An NFT, or Non-Fungible Token, represents a unique digital item or piece of content on the blockchain. Tokens like Bitcoin or Ether are fungible and are interchangeable. Each NFT is unique and is not interchangeable. NFTs are often used to represent digital art and other digital goods, proving authenticity and ownership.

ICO (Initial Coin Offering)

ICO (Initial Coin Offering) is a relatively modern fundraising mechanism, where new cryptocurrency projects sell their underlying tokens to the public. Sometimes, this sale is done in exchange for established cryptocurrencies, for example, Bitcoin or Ether. Essentially, it is a type of crowdfunding specific to the blockchain and cryptocurrency world. With this type of crowdfunding, supporters (early investors) are provided with tokens that imply potential future gains.

Pros and Cons of Cryptocurrencies

Below are some key pros and cons of using cryptocurrencies. These pros and cons are described from the point of view of an average person, not involved in the informal (also known as "grey") economy. For the informal economy, pros and cons might be different, and the informal economy is one of the use cases for cryptocurrencies.

	Pros for an average user	Cons for an average user
Public-key cryptography	Disintermediation: there is no one to decide if you can do a transaction. You do not need to ask anyone for permission or comply with any procedures – opening a bank account, proving the source of your funds, etc.	There is an inherent risk for currency owners: the loss of their currency. If the private key is lost or stolen, you do not own your cryptocurrency anymore.
Anonymity / pseudonymity	Privacy: others will not know about your transactions.	Regulatory pressure: traditionally all governments have wanted to control money flows very closely.
Little regulation due to the peer-to-peer nature	You have the freedom to use your money as you see fit, with minimal restrictions. No negative influence from governments and Central banks – inflation, etc.	Less protection provided by authorities: for example, there is more fraud in this area (as opposed to traditional, also known as "fiat", currencies).

By "little regulation" above, it is meant that technically it is quite difficult for regulators (government) to control if and how cryptocurrencies are used. But many countries are introducing some strict rules and even banning cryptocurrencies.

How This is Changing the Industry

The major way in which cryptocurrencies disrupt the financial world is by eliminating the need for traditional intermediaries (for example, traditional retail banks and central banks) and enable peer-to-peer transactions. This revolutionizes the way people transact. Now they can build trust without banks and governments. Imagine you need to send some money to your friend in some remote part of the world. You do not need to ask anyone for permission. You only need, usually, your smartphone.

A crypto economy creates a lot of opportunities for other intermediaries, which help cryptocurrencies function, for example:

- crypto exchanges, that facilitating the exchange of cryptocurrencies into other cryptocurrencies or into traditional currencies, or
- for some cryptocurrencies, miners, that contribute their computing power and energy to the network, to add new blocks to a blockchain and to ensure these additions are accurate.

Potential Risks and Challenges

The main challenge that cryptocurrencies are facing is regulatory pressure. Traditionally, all governments have wanted to control money flows very closely. Governments want this control for many reasons: fighting tax evasion, terrorism, money laundering, and so on. Sometimes innovation happens much faster than slow governments can react. But when they react, they are quite powerful. Many governments across the world have been consistently applying new regulations. This created a lot of difficulties for the crypto economy.

The second major challenge of the crypto economy is the inherent risk for currency owners of losing their currency. Having the private key and keeping it confidential are two essential rules of owning cryptocurrencies. Both can be difficult. If the key is lost, you do not own your cryptocurrency anymore. If the key is stolen, now you are sharing your cryptocurrency with someone else. There is no easy solution to this problem.

Third, traditionally, one of the major problems owners of cryptocurrencies have been facing – unstable currency rates. Many "stablecoins" were introduced to solve this problem. Still, some major cryptocurrencies (for example, Bitcoin) are not "stablecoins" and their rate might fluctuate dramatically.

Quiz

QUESTION 1.

What is cryptocurrency?

A. Digital currency.
B. Decentralized digital currency based on blockchain and cryptography.
C. Centralized digital currency.

QUESTION 2.

Can I access and manage my cryptocurrency if I lost my private key?

A. Yes, I can access it via the blockchain – public records.
B. It depends.
C. No, I cannot.

QUESTION 3.

What is blockchain?

A. Blockchain is a system of records of transactions, in which the records are not publicly available.
B. Blockchain is a system of immutable records of transactions, in which the records are publicly available via a distributed database.
C. Blockchain is a system of records of transactions, in which the records are publicly available for the last 3 years in a single database.

QUESTION 4.

How do cryptocurrencies disrupt the world of traditional finance?

A. Cryptocurrencies eliminate the need for traditional intermediaries and enable peer-to-peer transactions.
B. Cryptocurrencies make traditional financial institutions more efficient.
C. Cryptocurrencies change the way users interact with the traditional financial institutions.

QUESTION 5.

What are the key challenges and problems faced by cryptocurrencies?

A. Regulatory scrutiny and pressure from authorities.
B. Competition among multiple cryptocurrencies for users.
C. Ability to change the history of transactions.

Companies and Communities to Follow

- Binance (https://www.binance.com) is one of the largest global cryptocurrency exchanges.
- Coinbase (https://www.coinbase.com) is a US-based cryptocurrency exchange and a set of tools for accessing the crypto economy.
- Ethereum Foundation (https://ethereum.org) is a non-profit organization dedicated to supporting the cryptocurrency Ether and related technologies.

People to Know About

- Satoshi Nakamoto – the father of Bitcoin, the first cryptocurrency. This is a fictitious person. This pseudonym is used by a person or group of people, who remains unknown.
- Nouriel Roubini – a US economist and a writer. He is one of the most outspoken and consistent crypto critics.
- Vitalik Buterin – a Russian-Canadian software developer and one of the most influential figures in the world of cryptocurrency. He is the inventor of cryptocurrency Ether.

Answers to Quiz

1. **Answer: B.** Answer A is not correct because not all digital currencies are cryptocurrencies. Answer C is not correct, because cryptocurrency is not centralized. Rather, decentralization is one of the pillars of cryptocurrencies.

2. **Answer: C.** No, you can only access the blockchain – public records – to see the history of transactions and balances. If you are not using an app or any other "intermediary" to store your private key (as assumed in this question), you will never regain access. This is one of the major risks of holding cryptocurrency: you may lose your money forever.

3. **Answer: B.** Blockchain is a system of immutable records of transactions, in which the records are publicly available via a distributed database.

4. **Answer: A.** The major way in which cryptocurrencies disrupt the financial world is by eliminating the need for traditional intermediaries (for example, traditional retail banks and central banks) and enabling peer-to-peer transactions.

5. **Answer: A.** Answer B is not correct. Although we can say that there is some competition among multiple cryptocurrencies for users, this is rather not a major challenge. Answer C is not correct, because one of the pillars of blockchain technology is the concept of immutable transaction history by design.

CHAPTER 3

Hyper-Personalization

"I am used to disappointment with our banking, but I take this new offer quite personally."

This chapter explains how financial institutions move toward ubiquitous hyper-personalized ("bespoke") offerings enabled by technology for their clients and prospective clients. These hyper-personalized offerings are used more and more often in retail banking, insurance, and other areas of finance. Modern technology allows financial institutions to offer near real-time financial services based on a deep understanding of clients' goals, situations, and preferences.

In this chapter

Definition

Hyper-personalization of financial services refers to the deep customization of financial services to meet the specific goals, situations, and preferences of individual customers or prospective customers. This is enabled by modern advanced technology, including big data, advanced data analytics, and machine learning that allows financial institutions to (1) gather a lot of near real-time data –including big data – about a customer, (2) analyze this data, and (3) quickly offer or deliver service that meets specific needs and preferences.

Hyper-personalization of financial services goes far beyond traditional personalization by leveraging modern technology; it allows financial institutions to deliver highly targeted and personalized experiences to their customers.

Example

Let's say you bought your home with a loan (mortgage), and 80% of the price has been paid by mortgage. Each month, you pay the bank an amount based on the annual rate of 4% stated in your agreement.

Since you bought your house, many things have changed: you have substantially raised your credit score, you got married, and the central bank has decreased interest rates. One retail bank analyzed your data and quickly offered you the preapproved, highly personalized offer to refinance your mortgage with an annual rate of 3.1%.

Basics of Hyper-Personalization

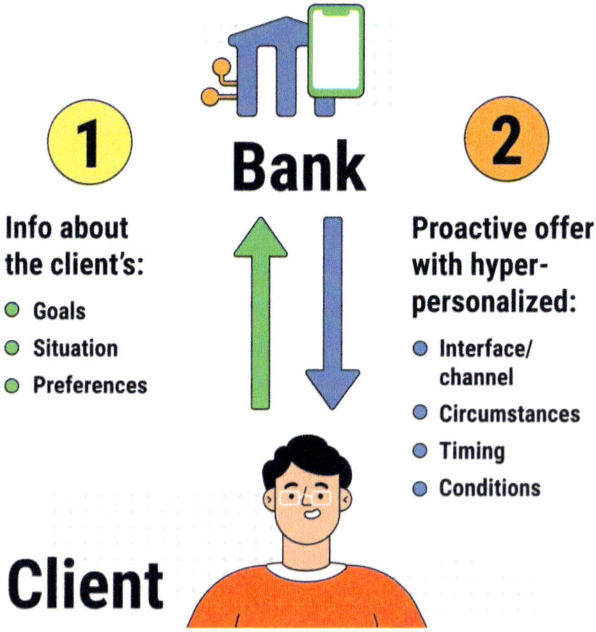

How do hyper-personalized offers typically work? First, the bank (or other financial institution) gathers information about the client's or prospective client's (1) goals, (2) situation, and (3) preferences. Then the bank (or other financial institution) proactively presents a hyper-personalized offer: (1) interface/ channel, (2) circumstances, (3) timing, and (4) conditions.

What We Usually Mean by Hyper-Personalization

What is important is the personalization of the main elements of the offerings, such as the percentage rate. Personalization was a part of financial services long before the advent of modern technology, such as big data and machine learning. For instance, even 100 years ago, when people received a letter from a bank, each client's name was on the envelope. Was this personalization?

Yes. Was it hyper-personalization? In a way, yes, because each envelope bore a different name. However, this is not the hyper-personalization that we discuss in this chapter; it is not the kind that is transforming banking and financial services today.

Key Elements of Hyper-Personalization

What are the key elements of the hyper-personalization approach? It focuses on addressing the specific goals, situations, and preferences of individual customers:

- Goals. Examples: Getting a car loan or refinancing a mortgage.
- Situation (circumstances). Examples: Age, religion, disabilities, etc.
    - Reputation is an important aspect of the "situation" category. Examples include having a relatively poor credit rating or impeccable transaction history.
    - Timing also plays a significant role in this category. For example, a customer might want to buy a car and finalize the deal within the next two weeks.
- Preferences. Example: A customer who wants to access insurance information through a convenient app and cares deeply about the simplicity and usability of the app. He is willing to accept a slightly higher percentage rate from a "convenient" company offering an excellent user experience and allowing payments through an app.

In the hyper-personalization approach, proactivity, preapproval, convenience, and ease of the channel and execution are also typically emphasized:

- Proactivity. Financial institutions proactively reach out to potential customers with offerings.
- Preapproval. Offerings are preapproved, which means that a potential customer doesn't need to apply and then wait for a decision while their information is analyzed, and a decision is made on whether to offer a service.

- Convenient channel and easy process. Hyper-personalization is most effective when combined with convenience in execution, requiring minimal effort from the consumer. For example, prepopulated documents in a user-friendly app where all tasks can be completed online with just a few clicks.

How might these "elements" relate to our previous example? Let's look at another example. The bank proactively reached out via an SMS or a WhatsApp message, recognizing that the prospective customer's mortgage was substantial. The bank proposed refinancing through a preapproved, highly personalized offer with a lower annual interest rate. This transaction can be finalized within the bank's mobile app.

Preapproval is Very Important

It is crucial for a hyper-personalized offer to be preapproved. When a financial institution analyzes users' data, it aims to answer three questions:

- Which offer best suits the customer? This maximizes the likelihood that the customer will accept the offer.
- Which offer will yield the most profit? This aims to maximize the profits of the financial institution.
- Can this product or service be offered to this customer?

The third question is of paramount importance and is often overlooked. In the realm of low-tech, traditional finance, it's common for a situation like the following to arise: A bank advertises a new credit card with an extended credit limit. You apply only to discover that, unfortunately, you aren't approved for this offer due to issues with your employment, credit rating, and so on. This blanket approach is far from hyper-personalized. In today's era of hyper-personalized finance, offerings must be preapproved to remain competitive.

Stages and Layers of Hyper-Personalization

For hyper-personalization to work, it is important to:

1. get data about the customer or prospective customer
2. analyze this data efficiently
3. have all systems ready to execute the offer effectively.

Efficient execution is neither (a) cost-prohibitive nor (b) confusing to customers. Both often could be the case because of the complexity of the system.

True efficient hyper-personalization happens on all organizational "layers" of financial organization, not only on the frontend. The personalization that is easiest for banks to implement and for customers to notice is usually about user experience, including the interface. But for hyper-personalization to work, all layers (including the backend) should support this approach.

Sources of Information

For hyper-personalized products and services, financial institutions need, first of all, to get a lot of data about the customer (or prospective customer). Perhaps they need as much customer data as possible to understand the customer as well as they can. The source of this information might not necessarily be the customers themselves. There might be others (third parties): companies, authorities, or even open sources, like social media.

Types of Information Sources

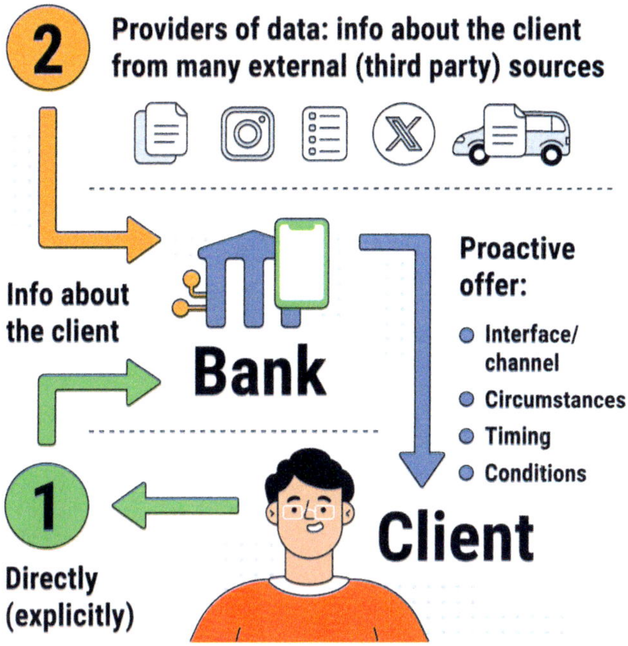

Let's look at two different types of information sources. A bank gathers customer information when customers give their details to the bank. Within this type, there is the customer's history, for example, his transactions. A bank also gathers information from multiple third parties, such as credit history from credit bureaus or driving records from authorities.

Event-Driven Products or Services

Hyper-personalized products and services might be driven by events, such as the customer's (or prospective customer's) actions or changes in market conditions.

Proactive Offer Triggered by an Event

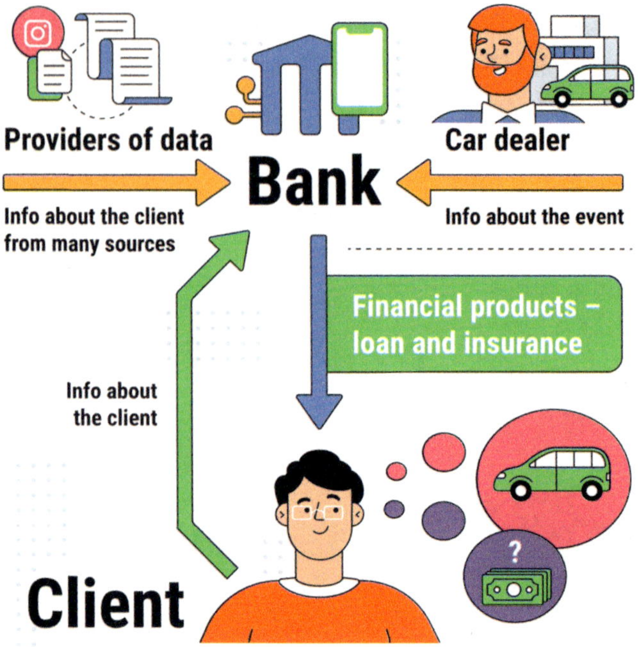

The above figure is an example of a proactive offer triggered by an event. The client is considering buying a car. With the client's consent, the car dealer shares this information with the bank. The bank proactively contacts the client and offers two event-driven hyper-personalized financial products: a car loan and car insurance.

Types of Data

Financial companies use various types of data to understand their customers as a basis for hyper-personalization. It doesn't necessarily have to be financial history, financial reputation, or financial health data like previous transactions, credit score, etc. It could include different types of information.

For example, it might be the case that how careful you are when driving or how proactively you monitor your health are good predictors of your financial behavior and tastes. Financial companies are working on proprietary models that use various types of data to understand the customer better than competitors.

Another example of non-financial data is smartphone-related behavior. How you use your smartphone, which apps you download, etc., says a lot about you. This smartphone-related behavior is easy to observe and quantify. Many financial companies try to come up with hundreds of various metrics to learn more about you.

One of the most important concepts and technologies in this regard is big data. Big data does not only mean large amounts of information, but volumes of data so large that it is impossible to efficiently analyze data using traditional methods. For example, many people have a substantial public presence on social media: likes, comments, and so on. These digital traces might reveal a lot of traits about people that companies can gather and analyze with big data technology.

What Drives Hyper-Personalization

Major drivers of the adoption and growth of the hyper-personalization approach are (1) the rapid development of several fields of technology, primarily AI (Artificial Intelligence) and machine learning, advanced data analytics, and big data analytics, (2) the increasing availability of data, and (3) competition. AI and machine learning will play the most important role in technology. These technologies will enable increasingly sophisticated and efficient tools to:

1. gather abundant near real-time data, including big data, about a customer or potential customer
2. analyze this data
3. swiftly offer and deliver the service to meet the specific needs and preferences.

Big data analytics and advanced analytics are two other technological pillars of hyper-personalization in finance. These tools allow financial institutions to process a large amount of useful data and extract valuable insights from it.

Advancement of some other technologies is also significant in hyper-personalization.

For example, augmented reality (AR) plays an important role in creating the basis for a personalized user experience for interaction with your financial institution. Imagine that you would like to visit the Bahamas branch of your bank and want your financial advisor there to look like your favorite Hollywood actor. This will be easy for the bank of the future – in fact, it may be part of the standard package.

Increased penetration of the Internet of Things (IoT) into our lives is another example of technology that will drive the hyper-personalization approach. Internet of Things will increase the amount of data about us that financial institutions can easily access from Internet of Things devices.

How Hyper-Personalization is Changing the World of Finance

Many customers would like – and already expect – their bank to know everything about them. Additionally, they expect their bank to act based on that knowledge. Many customers have always wanted as much personalization as possible. Now, technology makes this possible.

Technology democratizes bespoke banking. Let's consider my example of personalized mortgage refinancing. Even without modern technology, a very experienced and knowledgeable personal financial advisor whose only job is to monitor the mortgage market and your mortgage will come close for you. Technology makes this possible for almost everyone.

Ubiquitous hyper-personalization will become standard. Competition will drive this approach to become ubiquitous. Financial institutions must adopt it to survive. This creates opportunities for both disruptive start-ups and established companies capable of reinventing themselves.

Potential Risks and Challenges

Overall, hyper-personalization in finance has tremendous potential. However, privacy and data security will continue to be major challenges. This includes customers' concerns about their data privacy. To enable a hyper-personalized approach, financial institutions need to acquire and store a lot of customer data, including data that some customers consider quite sensitive. This data might be stolen or exposed due to negligence or cyberattacks. This is why data security issues and data privacy are of concern.

Large amounts of data gathered from various sources, cleaned up, and stored in one place in a structured way is a lucrative target for criminals. Cybersecurity is increasingly important to ward off this threat.

Regulators must respond to this problem by introducing new regulations to protect consumers. These new regulations themselves might pose a challenge for hyper-personalization, potentially slowing down progress.

Another challenge is that financial institutions' extensive knowledge about us and their ability to act incredibly quickly and shrewdly creates opportunities for manipulation. The aim of a bank (or any other financial institution) is to generate profits. This is why it's sometimes their job to convince us to make suboptimal financial decisions. Entities that know a lot about a customer do not necessarily use this information to find the best solutions for the customer.

Quiz

QUESTION 1.

What is hyper-personalized finance?

A. An approach that offers tailored financial products and services based on a customer's goals, situations, and preferences.
B. An approach that offers personalized recommendations.
C. An approach that focuses on creating customized user experiences.

QUESTION 2.

Would offering a different mortgage rate based solely on your credit score be an example of hyper-personalization enabled by financial technology?

A. Yes, because the mortgage rate isn't the same for all customers.
B. No. It could definitely be considered "personalization," but is an old way of personalization that has existed for as long as the concept of a mortgage has existed.
C. It depends on what technology was leveraged to arrive at the mortgage rate offered.

QUESTION 3.

Which of the following technologies is most commonly used in hyper-personalized banking?

A. Virtual reality.
B. Advanced data analytics and big data.
C. Blockchain.

QUESTION 4.

Which of the following answers best describes the drivers of hyper-personalization?

A. Regulatory pressures.
B. Rapid development of several fields of technology, increasing availability of data, and competition.
C. Emerging blockchain and cryptocurrency technology.

QUESTION 5.

Which of the following is a key challenge for the development and growth of the hyper-personalized finance approach?

A. High competition between financial institutions.
B. High hardware costs of enabling efficient, advanced data analytics and big data systems.
C. Data security issues and data privacy, including customers' concerns regarding their data privacy.

Companies to Follow

- Credit Karma (https://www.creditkarma.com) is a US-based personal finance company. It started out offering information about credit scores before adding more services. Now, Credit Karma includes personalized financial product options from third-party providers based on the information that Credit Karma accumulates about its users.
- Neobanks. Many neobanks are much more active than traditional banks in offering hyper-personalized financial offerings to their customers.

Answers to Quiz

1. **Answer: A.** B and C are parts of what hyper-personalized finance is about: recommendations and user experiences are facets of what is being customized. Option A better describes the range of what is being customized – products and services. Recommendations and user experiences are considered for this question as examples of financial products and services.

2. **Answer: B.** It could definitely be considered "personalization," but is an old way of personalization that has existed for as long as the concept of a mortgage has existed. There is most likely no advanced modern technology involved in setting rates for different credit score brackets.

3. **Answer: B.** Virtual reality and blockchain can both be leveraged to offer tailored financial products and services, but advanced data analytics and big data are used in hyper-personalized banking most often. It is one of the foundations of the hyper-personalization approach.

4. **Answer: B.** The major drivers are (1) the rapid development of several fields of technology, (2) the increasing availability of data, and (3) competition.

5. **Answer: C.** High competition between financial institutions is a driver, not an impediment, for the growth of the hyper-personalized finance approach. There are hardware costs associated with the enablement of efficient advanced data analytics and big data systems, but the major challenge in hyper-personalized finance is data security issues and data privacy, including customers' concerns regarding their

data privacy. To enable a hyper-personalized approach, financial institutions need to acquire and store a lot of customer data, including data that some customers consider quite sensitive and that might be stolen or exposed due to negligence or cyberattacks. This is why data privacy is a concern.

CHAPTER 4

Open Banking

"Honey, I am really concerned about our money in the bank. Do you think at least during the night the doors will be locked?"

This chapter explains what open banking is and how it changes the world of financial services. The chapter covers what drives open banking development, the opportunities open banking brings, and answers what the key challenges faced in advancing the open banking concept are.

In this chapter

What Open Banking Is

Open banking is the banking model in which banks are required to share customers' data upon customers' request. The government plays an important role in this model by exerting regulatory pressure aimed at ensuring financial institutions make data available via an API (Application Programming Interface). Open banking enhances competition and gives customers ownership over their own data.

Open finance is an extension of the open banking concept. Beyond just banking, it encompasses areas such as open insurance, open investments, and so on.

Example

Let us look at the following example. You instruct your bank to share the information about your transactions with a financial technology company. You would like to use the services of that financial technology company. The company now has your historical data to provide these services.

A common scenario in the current data exchange landscape is as follows. Established financial institutions with a long history provide data. Due to their longstanding operations, these traditional entities typically possess a wealth of customer data. Newer market entrants – young and technologically advanced challengers – receive data. These challengers deliver better user experiences due to their technological prowess. However, what they often lack is historical user data.

However, other possible combinations exist, such as two traditional banks sharing information among themselves.

Open Banking: Basics

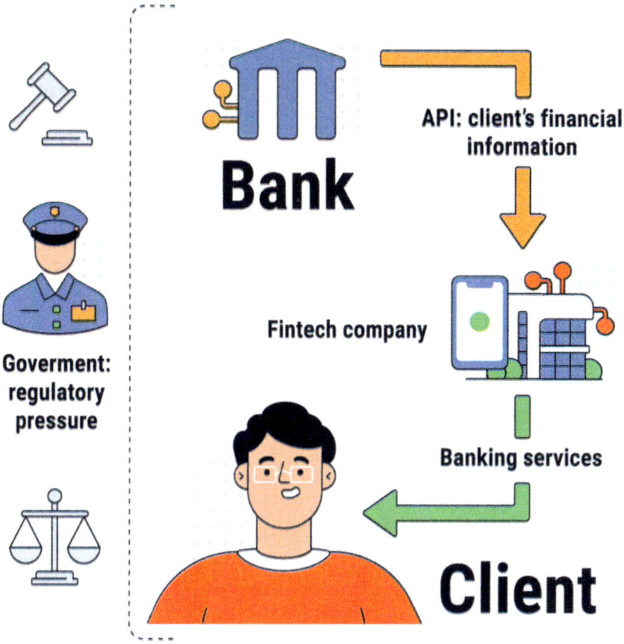

The above figure is an example of how open banking works. The government establishes a regulatory framework: your bank is required to open your data for you. Your bank creates an API (Application Programming Interface) to provide access to your data. A modern fintech company introduces a service via a mobile app, which your traditional bank doesn't offer: an "automated financial advisor." With this app, you can easily view information about your transactions. This fintech company retrieves your data from the bank via an API.

Two Scenarios of Open Banking

Open banking operates under various scenarios. Two typical scenarios are described below.

Scenario 1: Products and Services.

In this scenario, users instruct their primary bank (Bank 1) to share their financial data with another institution, such as a neobank (Neobank 2). Neobank 2 then leverages this imported data to provide the user with a specific product or service. For example, Neobank 2 might extend a credit card offer to the user. What makes the offer particularly appealing is that the favorable conditions or terms of the credit card are influenced by the user's transaction history from Bank 1.

Scenario 2: Comparative Analysis.

In this scenario, users authorize their bank (Bank 1) to transmit their financial data to a different platform or application (Application 2). This platform assesses the user's data and compares the services and products provided by Bank 1 with those from other financial institutions. For example, Application 2 might offer a comparative overview of credit card fees, showing how the rates of a credit card from Bank 1 compare against similar cards in the market.

Scenarios

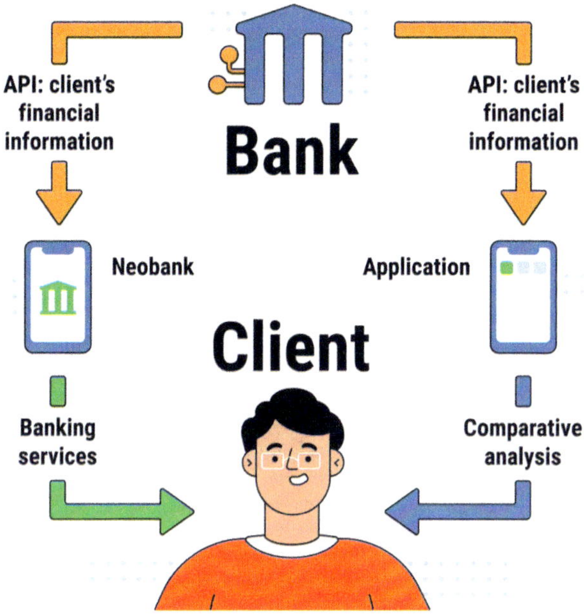

Scenario 1: a neobank provides the user with a specific product or service. Scenario 2: an application provides the user with a comparative analysis of financial products or services.

Why Open Banking is Important

Open banking promotes competition and limits detrimental industry concentration. Open banking gives users more control over their data. It transforms the world of finance. This transformation is particularly beneficial for new startups entering the market. Essentially, open banking diminishes one of the longstanding competitive advantages of traditional financial institutions: their vast reserves of customer data. Open banking provides opportunities for new players and business models.

Open Banking Limits Concentration

Open banking limits detrimental industry concentration. Open banking levels the playing field by diminishing one of the longstanding competitive advantages of traditional financial institutions: their vast reserves of customer data.

What API is and Why it is Important

In the context of open banking, a very important concept is the API (Application Programming Interface). An API allows in practice the portability of information. An API is a set of rules, protocols, and standards that enable different software applications to communicate with each other. An API allows one organization to get customer information from another organization in real time. It provides predefined programming functions and methods, enabling software developers to access and retrieve specific data.

How Open Banking is Different From Banking-as-a-Service

Open banking and banking-as-a-service (BaaS) both revolve around organizational interactions and leveraging APIs, facilitating the sharing of user data. However, there are two major differences between the two concepts.

1. In open banking, the primary focus is on data exchange. Organizations share and access financial data through standardized APIs. Bank-as-a-service goes a step further than just data exchange. In addition to information sharing, one entity typically outsources the actual execution of a service to another.
2. Secondly, in open banking, the data is shared among financial organizations. Whereas in a bank-as-a-service setup, one of the interacting parties is often not a financial institution. To illustrate, let us consider the initiation of payments within social networks. In this example, a user wants to transfer some money to his friend. Beyond just exchanging information between the social network and the bank, the social network leverages the bank's infrastructure to process the payment. The social network, in this case, is not a financial institution. However, some experts would see this as an example of open banking and classify this example under open banking.

What Drives Open Banking

Regulatory pressure serves as the primary driver of open banking. Contrary to many other areas of financial technology, regulatory pressure significantly influences the momentum of open banking. Regulators are propelling the industry by implementing rules that require financial institutions to essentially transfer their hold on data. These regulations are designed to empower customers by ensuring data portability, effectively allowing customers to possess and control their own financial data. As a result, customers can seamlessly transfer their banking information to different entities. These entities provide customers with a wider array of services, products, and enhanced user experiences.

How Open Banking is Changing the World of Finance

Open banking has emerged as a significant disruptor of traditional finance. It is fundamentally changing how customers access financial products and services, enhancing competition and opening up many new opportunities for consumers. The open banking concept aims to enhance the variety and quality of financial offerings available to the public.

As open banking reshapes the financial landscape, it presents significant opportunities for both new startups entering the market and established companies ready to reinvent their approach. This transformation is particularly beneficial for new startups entering the market. Open banking diminishes one of the longstanding competitive advantages of traditional financial institutions: their data.

Potential Challenges

Historically, data security has been one of the major challenges in the financial sector. The nature of finance inherently involves dealing with vast amounts of sensitive data, making it a prime target for breaches. With the emergence of open banking, this challenge has magnified. Open banking introduces APIs (Application Programming Interfaces), which are systems specifically designed to share data. Now, the primary defense against unauthorized access is to ensure that the data recipient has the necessary approvals, both from the customer and from regulatory standpoints. In essence, open banking, by its very design to facilitate information sharing, introduces a new layer of vulnerability.

Secondly, there is a question of user comprehension. Do users genuinely understand what they are consenting to? It is crucial that the user authorizes the data transfer and the user has control over this data. This means that a third party can access the data only if the customer really wants it to have it. Imagine a lengthy document presented in a tiny font with numerous pages. Would you read it in full before authorizing the data transfer?

This presents two significant challenges for regulators.

1. Ensuring that financial organizations not only formally open their data but also provide efficient tools (APIs) that are functional in practice.
2. Limiting and controlling how recipients use the data while ensuring these restrictions are not overly stringent. It is crucial to strike the right balance so as not to destroy the benefits of open banking by excessive limitations.

Quiz

QUESTION 1.

What is the key driver of open banking?

A. Demand for better services from customers.
B. Governments' pressure via changes in regulations.
C. Inability of large financial institutions to innovate and offer state-of-the-art banking services.

QUESTION 2.

Are open banking landscapes the same around the globe?

A. In a sense, they are similar, but regulation is different in different parts of the globe. The regulation and regulatory framework are important drivers shaping the industry. So, banking landscapes might be quite different around the globe.
B. Open banking landscapes are very similar around the globe. The only differences arise due to the differences in culture.
C. Open banking landscapes are the same around the globe.

QUESTION 3.

What is the best example illustrating how open banking works?

A. Under regulatory pressure, a large traditional bank must make customers' data available via API (Application Programming Interface). A neobank uses this data to offer the customers a better user experience and some products that are not offered by the large "old school" bank.
B. A large "old school" bank makes customers' data available via API (Application Programming Interface). Customers are now able themselves to download their own data and use it in any way they want.

C. A neobank makes its customers' data available. Customers are now able themselves to download their own data and bring this data to the new bank where they would like to open an account.

QUESTION 4.

Does open banking promote competition among financial institutions?

A. No. Open banking brings some positive impact to the world of finance. But it does not promote competition because it makes it harder for new challenger companies to compete.
B. No. Open banking brings some positive impact to the world of finance. But it does not promote competition, and promoting competition was not one of the aims of the open banking environment.
C. Yes, and promoting competition is one of the aims of regulators in promoting an open banking framework. In the open banking environment new financial institutions can more easily compete with traditional institutions, because the advantage of a traditional institution in having the historical user's data is removed.

QUESTION 5.

What is the primary risk and challenge for open banking's evolution?

A. Data security and data privacy. The open banking system entails financial institutions creating APIs (Application Programming Interfaces) for third parties. This creates opportunities for unauthorized access and data breaches.
B. Opposition of financial institutions to the implementation of the open banking system.
C. Increased costs, because additional hardware and software are necessary for creating an open banking framework.

Companies to Follow

- Finicity (https://www.finicity.com) is a US-based software company that offers API (Application Programming Interface) suites for developers working in several areas of finance and banking.
- Plaid (https://www.plaid.com) is a US-based software company that builds an open banking platform. This platform facilitates data transfers that enable fintech product.
- Yodlee (https://www.yodlee.com) is one of the leading data aggregation and data analytics platforms. It assists financial institutions in gathering a unified view of their customers from various sources and in offering better products and services based on the consolidated data.

People to Know About and to Follow

- Henry Chesbrough is a US scientist, who according to many sources coined the term "open innovation." "Open banking" initially was introduced as a part of the "open innovation" concept.

Answers To Quiz

1. **Answer: B.** Whereas open banking does bring some better services and more innovation, the right answer would rather be B. Because during the last decades the major force that drove open banking was governments changing regulations.

2. **Answer: A.** Open banking landscapes are not the same around the globe. Culture definitely affects everything. But the major difference in open banking landscapes comes from differences in regulatory frameworks.

3. **Answer: A.** A describes in a nutshell one of the simplified examples of how open banking works. B and C are not how open banking works.

4. **Answer: C.** A and B are not true.

5. **Answer: A.** To some extent, B and C might be correct. But definitely, data security and data privacy are the main risk and challenge for the development of the open banking system.

CHAPTER 5

Banking-as-a-Service

"You know what, I will outsource some parts of my infrastructure to enable cashless payments."

This chapter explains what banking-as-a-service (BaaS) is and why it is one of the key areas shaping the modern world of financial technology. The chapter covers several important banking-as-a-service concepts, including embedded finance and API (Application Programming Interface). The chapter discusses what drives banking-as-a-service development, what opportunities banking-as-a-service brings, and highlights the key challenges it faces.

In this chapter

What Banking-as-a-Service Is

Banking-as-a-service (BaaS) is a model of financial services in which one company that offers a service to customers outsources many components of this financial service from a third party. These behind-the-scenes components might include some key aspects, including technical and legal. This "third party" is the provider of banking-as-a-service.

Example

Let us imagine a situation where you would like to send money to your friend on a social network. First of all, you do not know any of this person's banking details – such as bank account number, and so on. Secondly, you do not want to waste your time switching to the banking app to make this transaction. So, you just use the "Send money" option within this social network with a couple of clicks. The social network itself does not have the infrastructure (the technical capabilities) to move money from one person to another and the banking license. The social network uses a "third party" as the provider of banking-as-a-service.

Basics of Banking-as-a-Service

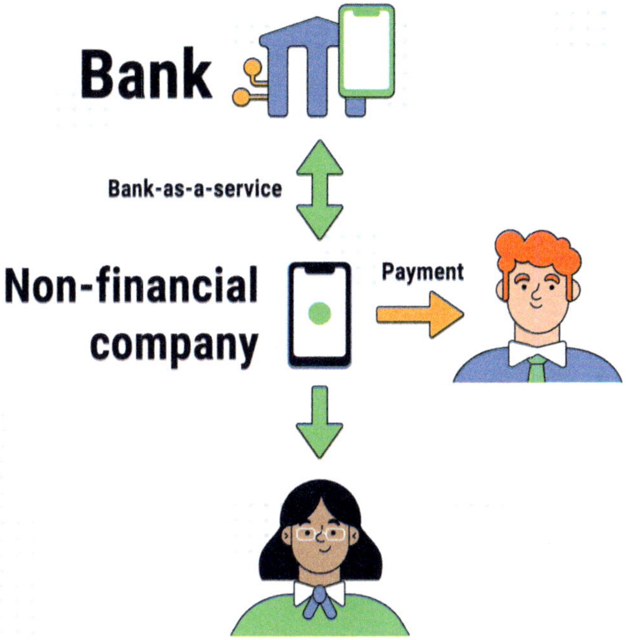

The above figure demonstrates how banking-as-a-service works. A non-financial company offers a financial service (for example, a payment). In this service, many components are outsourced behind the scenes from a financial company (for example, a bank). This financial company is the provider of banking-as-a-service.

How Banking-as-a-Service Works

Banking-as-a-service introduces a new model to the world of financial services. In this model, the frontend and the backend are divided between two providers: "front-end provider" and "back-end provider." This model adds flexibility to the way financial products and services can be offered.

The front-end provider is usually the company that is willing to find the potential end users, to understand their needs, and offer a specific user experience. This company outsources many components of this financial service from a third party. Usually, this company does not have a license for financial services. In a sense, the front-end provider resells the services under the white label.

The back-end provider is usually the financial company that is willing to organize technical infrastructure (capabilities) and license for financial services. This company does not directly sell financial services to the end user. Instead, it leverages the front-end provider to be an intermediary between the back-end provider and the end user.

The third type of player that is possible in this model is the company that offers the technical infrastructure. This technical infrastructure typically includes APIs (Application Programming Interfaces) that help the front-end provider and the back-end provider to connect.

The fourth "layer" in this "ecosystem" is the end user.

Typical Scenarios

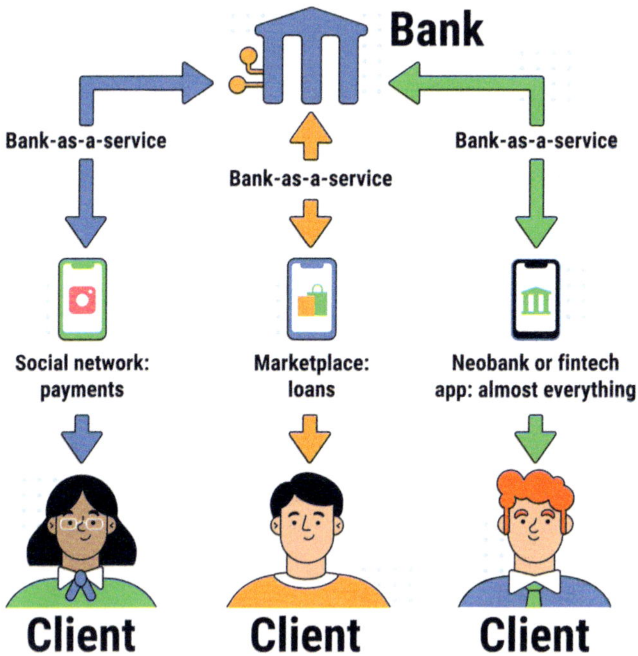

These are some of the typical current and future banking-as-a-service (BaaS) scenarios. The social network can offer users to pay each other. A marketplace offers loans, so that this loan might finance a deal on the marketplace. A neobank or fintech application offers a set of banking services without a banking license.

Banking-as-a-Service and Neobanks

The concept of banking-as-a-service is very much related to neobanks. Some neobanks are just intermediaries between the banks and the consumers. These neobanks offer banking services, but they do not have banking licenses. They use the licensed banks' APIs (Application Programming Interfaces) that provide banking-as-a-service.

API

In the context of banking-as-a-service, a very important concept is the API (Application Programming Interface). API allows, in practice, the portability of information. An API is a set of rules, protocols, and standards that allow different software applications to communicate with each other. API allows one organization to get information from another organization in real time. API provides predefined programming functions and methods, enabling software developers to access and retrieve specific data.

Embedded Finance

"Banking-as-a-service" and "embedded finance" are similar and closely related concepts. Both concepts are about integrating financial companies' financial services into a third-party platform or application. The banking-as-a-service concept usually refers to the process and infrastructure. The embedded finance concept usually means the resulting product or service itself.

White Label

In the context of banking-as-a-service, an important concept is the "white label." The "white label" concept in business refers to a model in which the product or service is produced by one company but rebranded and sold by another company. The company that sells the product uses its own brand. This concept applies to the world of financial services as well. The term "white label" refers to the idea that a product has a blank label, which can be filled by the company that sells the product to the end user. With the banking-as-a-service concept, the back-end providers sell financial products and services with a "white label."

Classification of Banking-as-a-Service

Banking-as-a-service is a very flexible concept and allows for building various financial products and services. One of the ways to classify banking-as-a-service models is to divide this variety into two types:

- Type 1. A particular financial service (or less often several financial services) is embedded into the non-financial application, platform, and so on.
- Type 2. All products or services (or less often several products and services) of a neobank or fintech application are outsourced to a licensed financial company by this neobank or fintech application.

Two Types

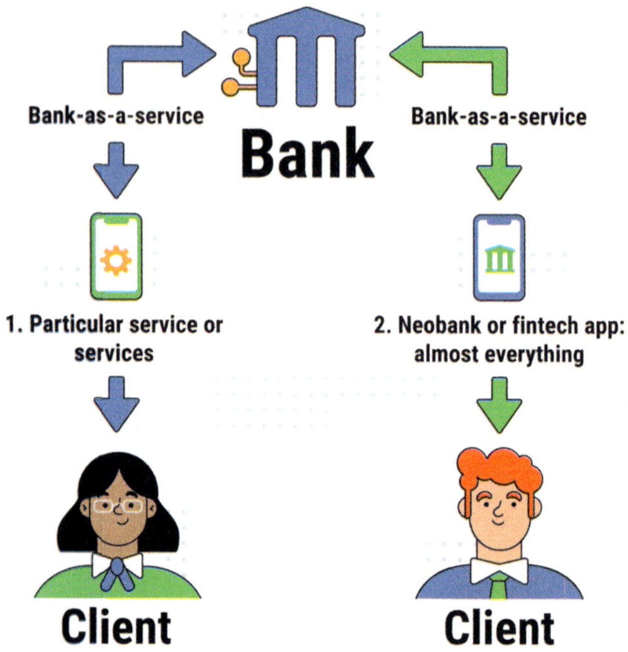

This figure shows the two key banking-as-a-service types. 1. A particular financial service (services) in non-financial application, platform, and so on. 2. All services (or several of them) of neobank or fintech application.

Banking-as-a-Service Ecosystem

In the banking-as-a-service model, beyond the fundamental entities of the back-end bank and front-end businesses leveraging the model, an ecosystem (or network) of various entities is emerging. Within this ecosystem, one of the key roles belongs to banking-as-a-service software platforms. These platforms serve as the essential intermediary technology enabling banks to extend their services.

This ecosystem might include more than one provider of banking-as-a-service. Front-end businesses can outsource financial products and services to different providers: one service to one provider, another service to another provider, and so on. Also, it is possible to combine various components outsourced to multiple providers into one front-end service.

Ecosystem

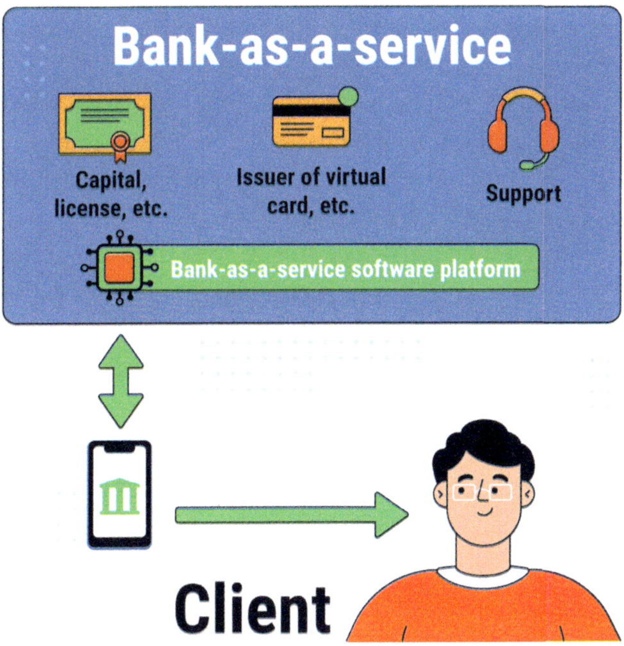

This is an example of a banking-as-a-service ecosystem. A software platform serves as the essential intermediary technology. Various components of financial services or products (such as capital, issuance of virtual credit card, support, etc.) are outsourced to multiple providers into an integrated front-end service.

Banking-as-a-Service vs. Open Banking

Banking-as-a-service and open banking both revolve around organizational interactions and leveraging APIs (Application Programming Interfaces), facilitating the sharing of user data. However, there are two major differences between the two concepts.

1. In open banking, the primary focus is on data exchange. Organizations share and access financial data through standardized APIs. Bank-as-a-service goes a step further than just data exchange. In addition to information sharing, one entity typically outsources the actual execution of a service to another.
2. Secondly, in open banking, the data is shared by financial organizations. In a bank-as-a-service setup, however, one of the interacting parties is often not a financial institution. To illustrate, let us consider the initiation of payments within social networks. In this example, a user wants to transfer some money to his "friend". Beyond just exchanging information between the social network and the bank, the social network leverages the bank's infrastructure to process the payment. The social network, in this case, is not a financial institution. Although, some experts would see this as an example of open banking and classify this example under open banking.

Banking-as-a-Service vs. Banking-as-a-Platform

What is the difference between banking-as-a-service and banking-as-a-platform (BaaP)? Banking-as-a-platform is an entirely different concept. Banking-as-a-platform refers to an approach in financial services, where banks provide a technological platform for third parties to integrate their products into the bank's user experience. It is essentially a marketplace for services, with the bank acting as the infrastructure provider.

What Drives Banking-as-as-Service and Embedded Finance

The emergence of banking-as-a-service and embedded finance is driven, first of all, by customer demand. Customers increasingly expect convenient, personalized financial services. This is why companies are motivated to offer new and better financial experiences. Banking-as-a-service is one of the ways to do so.

Secondly, digitalization, modern technologies, and IT tools, have enabled banking-as-a-service and embedded finance. An important IT tool in this context is an API, which facilitates the fast, seamlessly delivered of financial services.

How This is Changing the Industry

How does banking-as-a-service change the industry? First, it creates banking experiences that did not exist before, for example, the ability to make payments within non-banking platforms, services, and applications. Secondly, it saves us time. For example, with payments, sometimes we can make a transaction without switching to the bank's app, trying to find recipient's banking details, and many other steps.

For users, banking-as-a-service creates a better user experience for the financial products and sometimes enables financial products that would not have been used without the banking-as-a-service model because they would have been too complex or not feasible at all.

For financial companies, banking-as-a-service gives opportunities to create new revenue streams by becoming banking-as-a-service providers. For non-banking companies, this provides an opportunity to add financial products to their products and services. For startups, banking-as-a-service gives tremendous opportunities as it enables them to launch products and services quickly – just by connecting to the API. There is one more group of companies that can benefit from developing banking-as-a-service – providers of technological platforms that connect various parties. Such technological platforms offer APIs that connect the banks and the companies that integrate financial products into their user experiences.

Potential Challenges

There are several key challenges in the development of banking-as-a-service.

Historically, data security has been one of the major challenges in the financial sector. The nature of finance inherently involves dealing with vast amounts of sensitive data, making it a prime target for breaches. With the emergence of banking-as-a-service, this challenge has magnified. Banking-as-a-service introduces APIs (Application Programming Interfaces), which are systems specifically designed to share data. Now, the primary defense against unauthorized access is ensuring that the data recipient has the necessary approvals, both from the customer and regulatory standpoints. In essence, banking-as-a-service introduces a new layer of vulnerability by its very design to facilitate information sharing.

Secondly, one of the key challenges is the complexity of integration. Banking-as-a-service often involves integrating multiple systems. These systems are often quite different and quite complex. At the same time, banking is an area where customers expect smooth and impeccable execution. For example, for payments, we do not expect the payments to go through in 90% of situations. We usually expect 100%.

The third key challenge that banking-as-a-service is facing is about regulatory hurdles. Traditionally, banking has always been quite a regulated industry. Sometimes, innovation happens much faster than slow governments can react. But when they react, they are creating some requirements that might be difficult to comply with.

Quiz

QUESTION 1.

Which of the following statements about banking-as-a-service is true?

A. Banking-as-a-service refers to the provision of brick-and-mortar banking branches. In this model, banks rent out their physical facilities to other organizations.
B. Banking-as-a-service refers to the model in which a bank outsources its entire banking operations to a third-party provider.
C. Banking-as-a-service refers to the model in which one company, offering a service to customers, outsources many components of this financial service from a third party.

QUESTION 2.

What is embedded finance?

A. Embedded finance is a concept referring to the situation in which a service is offered by two financial institutions together and one of them is, in a sense, embedded into the other.
B. Embedded finance is a concept referring to the financial landscape where financial institutions are parts of an overall interconnected financial system.
C. Embedded finance is a concept referring to the situation in which a financial product or service is integrated into a non-financial user experience.

QUESTION 3.

What is one of the potential beneficial consequences for the financial system of adopting banking-as-a-service?

A. Cost reduction, because the banking-as-a-service concept allows banks to outsource some operations to a third-party provider.
B. Better customer experience, because banking-as-a-service enables new banking experiences for customers.
C. Enhanced data security and data privacy with reduced level of fraudulent operations.

QUESTION 4.

What kind of opportunities does banking-as-a-service concept create for financial institutions, providers of banking-as-a-service?

A. Brand differentiation.
B. New revenue streams and expansion of service offerings.
C. Less complicated regulatory compliance.

QUESTION 5.

What are the key challenges in the development of the banking-as-a-service model?

A. Data security and data privacy, complexity of integration, and regulatory compliance.
B. High costs of hardware and a complex branding strategy.
C. Complexity for the customer, the end-user.

Companies to Follow

- Adyen (https://www.adyen.com/) is a Dutch-based financial technology company that offers a banking-as-a-service financial technology platform.
- Green Dot Corporation (https://www.greendot.com/) is a US financial technology company that develops and offers banking-as-a-service platform.
- Stripe (https://stripe.com/) is a global financial services company. Aside from other services Stripe offers banking-as-a-service APIs (Application Programming Interfaces) that enable other companies to embed financial services into their existing software.

Answers to Quiz

1. **Answer: C.** Choice C correctly describes what banking-as-a-service is about. Statements A and B are not true.

2. **Answer: C.** Option C accurately describes what embedded finance is.

3. **Answer: B.** In choice A, the statement about outsourcing is wrong: the banking-as-a-service concept is not about banks being able to outsource some operations to a third-party provider. Option C is wrong, because data security and data privacy are rather some of the key challenges in the development of banking-as-a-service. This is because banking-as-a-service might create opportunities for unauthorized access and data breaches.

4. **Answer: B.** It is unlikely that banking-as-a-service would give a financial institution (provider) any opportunities to differentiate its brand (choice A) or to simplify regulatory compliance (choice C).

5. **Answer: A.** Choice A accurately describes three key challenges in the development of the banking-as-a-service model.

CHAPTER 6

Neobanks

"I would disagree that neobanking is convenient. I liked the old-school brick-and-mortar much more."

This chapter explains what neobanks are and how they are transforming the world of financial services. The chapter covers mostly retail banks, but also touches upon the concept of "neo everything" in financial services – neobrokers, etc. The chapter discusses what drives neobanking development, the opportunities neobanking brings, and highlights the key challenges it faces.

In this chapter

What Neobanks Are

Neobanks are banks that focus on remote service with superior digital user experience and are generally cost-effective.

Neobanks aim to provide a better online user experience compared to traditional banks. Sometimes, neobanks are referred to as "challenger banks" because they challenge traditional banks. Usually, neobanks are cost-effective for two main reasons. First, because of the remote model, they have no brick-and-mortar locations. Secondly, they have no legacy code and infrastructure. They can build more effective operational models because they are building them from scratch.

Example

You have downloaded the banking app onto your smartphone. You have done a couple of things remotely to prove that you are you: took a selfie and sent it to the bank, uploaded your documents (for example, a driver's license). And your bank is ready. You have your basic banking needs covered: a virtual payment card, a checking account, a savings account, and so on. You do not need to go to the bank's branch. This is how a neobank works.

Basics of Neobanking

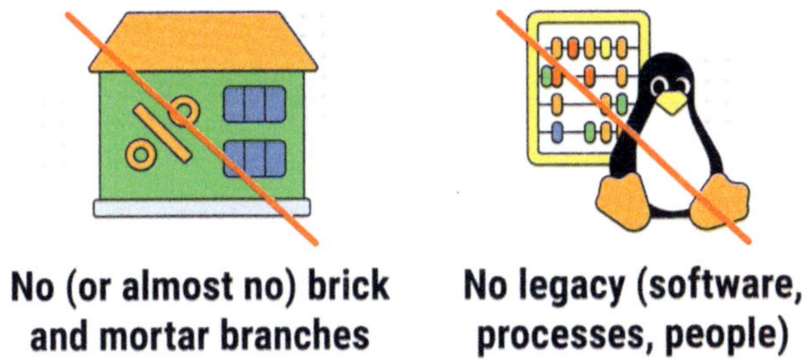

Neobanks are focusing on remote service. They have no legacy code and infrastructure and are able to build more effective operational models.

How Neobanks Work

Neobanks, also known as challenger banks, are reinventing banking. Banking has always been quite a conservative and slow-to-change industry. Now, modern technology has made disruption possible. Neobanks are setting new standards and are reinventing several aspects of banking:

- First, neobanks have no (or almost no) brick-and-mortar branches. This makes them very cost-effective. Maintaining brick-and-mortar branches is one of the substantial costs of a bank. A bank offering comparable products and services while having substantially lower costs makes it very competitive.

- Secondly, neobanks are focusing on modern technology and superior user digital experience. Nowadays, most of the traditional banks offer remote banking as well. However, neobanks' focus on a better online user experience (compared to traditional banks) often makes a difference. If a bank offers comparable products and services, for example, checking and savings accounts, while at the same time having a substantially more convenient user experience, it creates a competitive advantage.
- Third, neobanks are building everything from scratch. This means having no legacy: of code, infrastructure, or employees with outdated skills.
- Also, neobanks usually focus on products and services which are: (1) less balance sheet intensive (an example of a balance sheet intensive product is a mortgage or car loan), (2) more frequently used: payments, etc.

This makes neobanks cost-effective, convenient to the end users, and free from the reputation of old-fashioned, cumbersome, "so 20th-century" organization in the eyes of prospective clients.

Neo Everything

Like retail banking, there are similar trends in other finance areas. Many challengers offer "neo experiences" – in money management, brokerage, insurance, and so on. Nowadays, most traditional financial institutions offer remote financial services and converge to "neo" finance. "Neo" finance is becoming the new standard.

Classification of Neobanks

There are many ways to classify neobanks. One of the ways is to distinguish between three types:

Type 1. True bank. This bank has all the necessary licenses and infrastructure. Typically, it is a relatively new bank focusing on remote service with superior digital user experience.

Type 2. Rent-a-charter neobank. This is rather a banking app of a traditional banking institution. This application is not a bank itself. It relies on renting the regulatory and financial infrastructure of the bank.

Type 3. Built with BaaS. This type is very similar to type 2: type 3 neobank relies on renting the regulatory and financial infrastructure of the bank.

The difference between type 2 and type 3 is as follows.

In type 2, neobank is usually fully controlled by the traditional bank. In fact, the neobank might not even have a separate legal entity. It could just be an application for a traditional bank. Alternatively, the neobank can be organized as a separate legal entity, but fully controlled by the traditional bank.

In type 3, neobank is usually an arms-length partner of the traditional bank. The neobank is not fully controlled by the traditional bank. The neobank uses the banking-as-a-service concept to use the regulatory and financial infrastructure of the traditional bank. The neobank can change the provider (of banking-as-a-service) or use several providers simultaneously.

Three Types of Neobanks

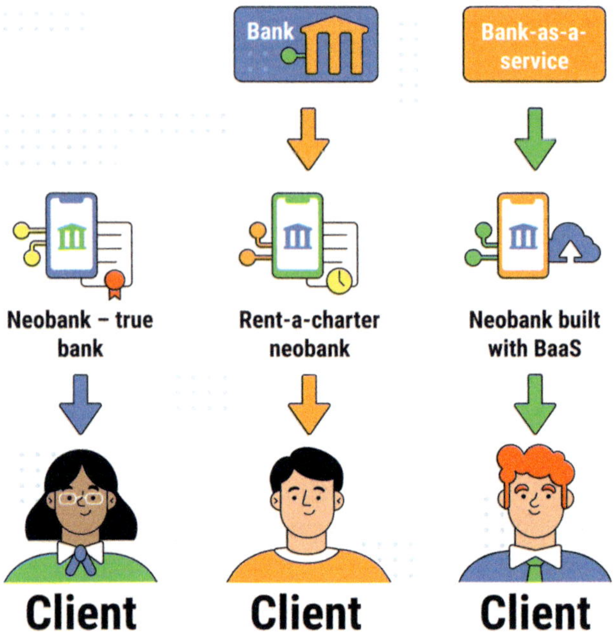

There are three types of neobanks: true bank, rent-a-charter neobank, built with banking-as-a-service (BaaS).

Examples of Type 2 and Type 3

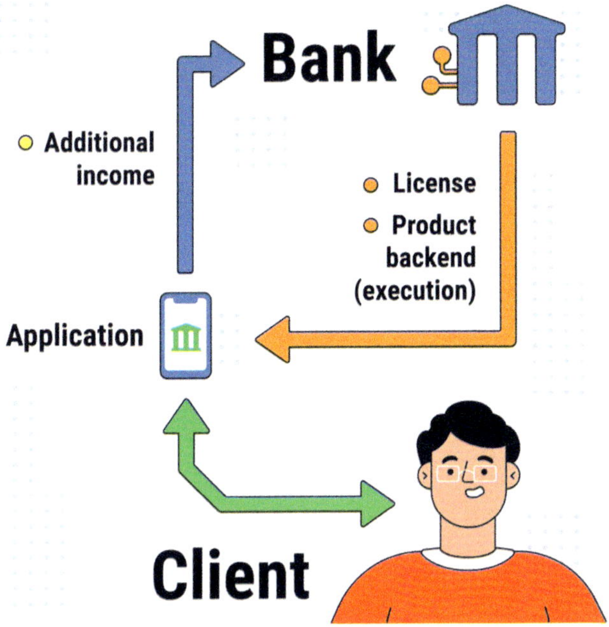

"Rent-a-charter" and "built with banking-as-a-service (BaaS)" neobanks. There are traditional banking institutions behind neobanks' brands and applications.

Why Building from Scratch is Efficient

Neobanks' ability to build everything from scratch according to modern best practices is often underestimated. Yet, it is one of the cornerstones of neobanking success. These are the examples of legacy and inertia that stand in the way of innovation:

- code (old software)
- aging infrastructure
- personnel with outdated skills
- contractual relationships that limit flexibility

Neobanks defeat this legacy and inertia by building many facets of their business from scratch.

Pros and Cons of Neobanks

Neobanks are different, and traditional banks are different as well. But for an average neobank and an average traditional bank, these are the key pros and cons of using neobank (vs. traditional bank) for a typical user.

Pros	Cons
• Better remote service and user experience • Wider range of remote services • Lower fees	• Lack of physical branches • Limited range of services

Range of Products

Neobanks and modern banks often have a more limited range of services than traditional banks. However, some neobanks and modern banks are trying to offer some products and services that traditional banks usually do not offer. They innovate and offer some novel offerings that would allow these banks to get a unique space in the financial ecosystem. Such products and services can be:

- financial products and services not typically offered by traditional banks, for example, credit score building
- relatively new financial products, for example, investing in cryptocurrencies
- non-financial products, for example, travel packages and tickets.

Some neobanks and modern banks even leverage the banking-as-a-platform (BaaP) model. Banking-as-a-platform refers to an approach in financial services where banks provide a technological platform for third parties to integrate their products into the bank's user experience. It is essentially a marketplace for services, with the bank acting as the infrastructure provider.

Banking-as-a-Service

Banking-as-a-service (BaaS) is an important concept in the context of neobanking for understanding some cases and aspects of neobanking. Banking-as-a-service is a model of financial services in which one company, which offers a service to customers, outsources many components of this financial service to a third party. These behind-the-scenes components might include some key elements, including technical and legal. This "third party" is the provider of banking-as-a-service.

How Neobanks Make Money vs. Old School Banks

Neobanks are different, and traditional banks are different as well. For an average neobank and an average traditional bank, these usually are the key differences in the way the banks make money:

Neobank: less (in share of income)	Neobank: more (in share of income)
• capital-intensive services and products, for example, mortgage • B2B (Business-To-Business) services, especially "complicated" services like investment banking	• interchange • fees (for transactions, and so on) • interest income

Interchange

Interchange is an important concept in the context of neobanking. Interchange is the fee paid by a merchant's bank to a cardholder's bank (issuer) for card transactions. Interchange compensates the issuer for the risks and costs it incurs. On average, for neobanks, the interchange fees are a much larger share of revenue as opposed to traditional banks. By optimizing their card offerings and encouraging card transactions, neobanks can generate substantial income from interchange.

What Drives Neobanking

A significant driver of neobanks development, similar to the development of many other areas of fintech, has been the widespread and affordable access to the Internet and smartphones. Now, smartphones (and computers) are affordable to almost everyone, and Internet connectivity is available almost everywhere around the world. These facts have facilitated the digitalization of many areas of our lives, including banking.

Also, neobanks have experienced significant growth in part due to the evolving regulatory environments. Regulators in many countries have made remote banking processes that once required physical presence possible. Innovations such as remote account opening, digital authentication, and online KYC (Know Your Customer) procedures have become acceptable due to regulatory changes.

How This is Changing the Industry

Neobanks bring better, more convenient banking experience to the users. Also, despite banking being a conservative industry, neobanks force traditional banks to innovate in order to survive in competition. Banking has always been a very slow industry. Some financial institutions are hundreds of years old. Now, neobanks disrupt this industry and set new standards.

This disruption creates significant opportunities for new players. They are more focused on technology than traditional players and can offer a better user experience with lower costs. Thus, they can compete successfully with traditional companies, attracting clients, particularly younger ones. These clients are either switching from traditional banks or beginning to use banking services for the first time in their lives.

Neobanking offers numerous job opportunities for IT (information technology) professionals: software developers, designers, user experience specialists, testers, and so on. While neobanking disrupts the profession of the banker, it creates more highly desired white-collar positions in the IT domain.

Potential Risks and Challenges

Neobanks' history is much shorter than the history of traditional banks. Neobanks are yet to build brands and reputations, which are very important in the world of finance. Many customers trust traditional banks more. This neobanks' lack of trust and reputation is a hurdle in their development. Many potential customers have seen neobanks as early-stage startups, the majority of which will not survive. So, they are not to be trusted. This perception is changing steadily as many neobanks are now rather strong, dynamic, established, yet young, companies rather than startups.

Another key challenge that neobanks are facing is regulatory hurdles. Traditionally, banking has always been quite a regulated industry. Sometimes, innovation happens much faster than slow governments can react. But when they react, they are creating some requirements that might be difficult to comply with.

Quiz

QUESTION 1.

What are neobanks?

A. Neobanks are banks that exist for a relatively short period of time as opposed to the traditional financial institutions.
B. Neobanks are the banks that usually offer financial products that are not capital intensive. For example, neobanks usually do not offer mortgages – this requires a lot of capital from the bank.
C. Neobanks are banks, that are focusing on remote service with superior digital user experience and are relatively cost effective.

QUESTION 2.

What is the key driver of neo banking expansion?

A. Widespread connectivity and rapid advancements in technology.
B. Overall economic conditions and economic growth.
C. Supportive regulatory environment.

QUESTION 3.

What is a key advantage of neobanks over traditional banks?

A. Wide network of physical branches.
B. Superior digital user-friendly experience.
C. Higher interest rates on savings and investment accounts.

QUESTION 4.

What is a key advantage of neobanks over traditional banks in terms of cost?

A. Neobanks are cost-effective because of the remote model and having no legacy code and legacy infrastructure to support.
B. Neobanks are cost-effective because of the higher brand recognition and awareness.
C. Neobanks are cost-effective because they have better access to capital.

QUESTION 5.

What are the key challenges of neobanks in their expansion?

A. Building customers' and potential customers' trust and brand recognition. Traditional banks with a long history are sometimes still more trustful in the eyes of many cautious customers.
B. Regulatory hurdles. Neobanks operate in a highly regulated industry. Some parts of remote user experience, for example remote identification and KYC (Know Your Customer) procedures, are challenging in terms of compliance.
C. Both A and B are correct.

Neobanks to Follow

- Chime (https://www.chime.com) is a US-based neobank. Chime is one of the leading neobanks in the US by number of users. It provides many services, including fee-free accounts and has emphasis on user-friendly interface.
- Revolut (https://www.revolut.com) is a UK-headquartered global neobank. Revolut is one of the largest and most successful neobanks globally. Revolut offers a range of financial services, including multi-currency accounts, international money transfers, prepaid debit cards, and so on. With its focus on low-cost transactions, a convenient digital user experience, and global accessibility, Revolut has gained significant popularity.
- Wise (https://www.wise.com), previously "Transferwise", is a UK-headquartered global neobank. Wise is one of the biggest neobanks globally. One of the key areas of Wise's focus is international transactions: Wise aims to offer low fees and attractive exchange rates.

People to Know About and to Follow

- Stanislav Storonsky is the CEO and co-founder of the UK-based global neobank Revolut. He frequently talks on the topic of neobanks and digital innovation in finance in general.
- Anne Boden is a former CEO and co-founder of the UK-based neobank Starling. She frequently talks on the topic of neobanks and digital innovation in finance in general.

Answers to Quiz

1. **Answer: C.** Statements A and B more or less correctly describe some neobanks' characteristics. But C gives the best definition.

2. **Answer: A.** Option B has nothing to do with the correct answer. Option C might be correct, because, definitely, for neobanks the new regulatory framework is needed. There have been some changes in the regulatory framework that have facilitated neobanks' existence and success. But the best answer is A, because this is the most impactful driver.

3. **Answer: B.** A wide network of physical branches is not an advantage, because usually neobanks do not have physical branches. It might be the case that a neobank offers higher interest rates compared to a traditional bank. But the key advantage is rather a superior digital user-friendly experience.

4. **Answer: A.** Neobanks are cost-effective for two main reasons: remote model and having no legacy code and legacy infrastructure. Options B and C do not accurately describe key advantages. Also, they are mostly untrue.

5. **Answer: C.** Both A and B are among the key challenges neobanks face.

CHAPTER 7

Crowdfunding

"Honey, maybe we should crowdfund our vacation? Or at least maybe you will also chip in?"

This chapter explains the concept of crowdfunding in the world of finance and banking: rewards crowdfunding, equity crowdfunding, crowdlending, and donations. This chapter describes how crowdfunding changes the world of finance. The chapter covers what drives the development of crowdfunding, the opportunities crowdfunding brings, and answers what the key challenges faced in advancing crowdfunding are.

In this chapter

What Crowdfunding Is

Rewards crowdfunding, equity crowdfunding, crowdlending, and donating are business models in finance, where an important aspect is the participation of a relatively large number of "players." These models are examples of crowdsourcing in which large numbers of participants make contributions. In this case, the participants' inputs are capital (funds). The "crowd" contributes money to the founders and/or managers of the project, company, or initiative.

Example

Imagine you want to open a cafe. You do not have money to start – to hire people, lease a space, and so on. There is no single person who is ready to give you enough money to start. This is why you started an online campaign and found several thousand enthusiasts who are willing to contribute relatively small amounts of money. This is crowdfunding.

Basics of Crowdfunding

A lot of enthusiasts are willing to contribute relatively small amounts of money.

How Crowdfunding Works

Modern crowdfunding is usually an Internet-enabled online process. This is why it is one of the areas that is heavily influenced by modern technology – the Internet and digitalization. However, other means of crowdfunding still exist: mail, fundraising events, and so on.

Crowdfunding is used for both for-profit and non-profit projects (as well as companies, initiatives, etc.).

The crowdfunding process usually has two groups of participants. The first group is individuals who manage the project and put their time and effort into it. They are usually also the founders. The second group is individuals who usually do not contribute time and effort but contribute funds. These are "supporters" or "backers."

The third important actor in the modern crowdfunding world is a platform. The modern online platforms allow founders to meet supporters. The platforms provide necessary technology, moderation, and checks.

Crowdfunding has traditionally been skewed towards more "emotional" projects appealing to many: artistic, creative projects, projects with a social impact, and so on.

Types

There are four major types of crowdfunding:

- Reward-based crowdfunding (also known as rewards crowdfunding or non-equity crowdfunding). In this type of crowdfunding, contributors of funds receive non-financial rewards in return. Rewards-based crowdfunding contributors do not receive equity in the company that gathers the funds, and the returns of contributors are not tied directly to the company's future profits.
- Equity-based crowdfunding (also known as equity crowdfunding or crowdinvesting). In this type of crowdfunding, contributors of funds receive equity in the company that gathers the funds. The contributors become shareholders.
- Debt-based crowdfunding (also known as crowdlending, peer-to-peer lending, or peer-to-peer loans). In this type of crowdfunding, contributors lend money and receive it back after some time with a pre-defined interest.
- Donation-based crowdfunding. In this type of crowdfunding, contributors donate money without the expectation of receiving anything in return.

Four Types of Crowdfunding

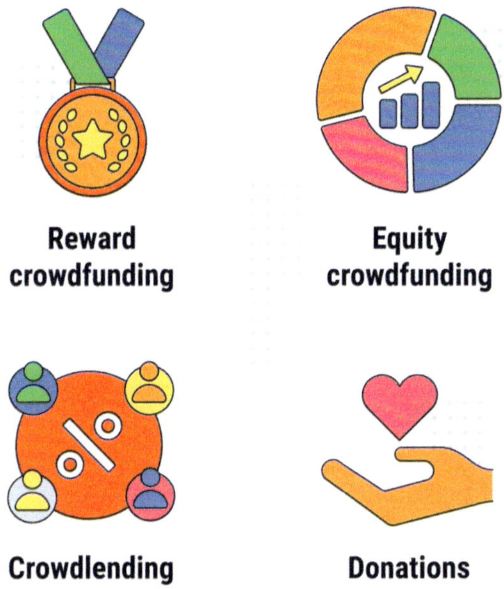

There are four major types of crowdfunding: reward crowdfunding, equity crowdfunding, crowdlending, and donations.

Reward Crowdfunding

In reward crowdfunding, supporters receive non-financial rewards in return for their contribution. Usually, supporters might be motivated by the potential reward itself. Secondly, supporters' motivation might be to help founders, a company, a product, or a cause to succeed.

In reward crowdfunding, typical supporters' rewards might be:

- products or prototypes of products
- exclusive content or exclusive experiences
- public acknowledgment and recognition

- merchandise
- free, early, discounted, or premium access to content, events, and so on.

Rewards are not financial and are not tied to the future company's (or project's) profitability. Otherwise, this would not be reward crowdfunding. In a way, rewards depend on the future success of the company or project. If a cafe is not opened, there will be no free dinners. If a musician does not finish the album, he will not be able to give supporters access to it. But these rewards are not tied to future profits. In other words, the size of the company or project's future profits (if there are any) will not change the rewards in any way.

Reward crowdfunding is not investing. This is why supporters are not usually professional investors or angel investors. Typical use cases are: music and movies, software, various types of inventions, various types of projects with social impact, and so on.

Reward Crowdfunding: Example

This is an example of reward crowdfunding. Supporters will receive only free dinners. They have contributed funds because (aside from getting dinners in return) they might like founders and would like to have this type of cafe in their neighborhood, and so on.

Equity Crowdfunding

In equity crowdfunding, supporters (investors) receive financial rewards in return for their contribution. Contributors receive equity in the company that gathers the funds. The contributors become shareholders. Usually, supporters are primarily motivated by this potential financial reward. A relatively minor part of supporters' motivation might be to help founders or a company to succeed.

Rewards are financial and are tied to the future company's success and profitability. This is very much different from reward crowdfunding. Equity crowdfunding in many countries is heavily regulated. One of the key reasons is investor protection. And investors need protection. First, fraudulent crowdfunding might happen. Secondly, even without fraud, statistics of startups tell that most startups do not bring any financial return to their investors.

Equity crowdfunding is essentially one of the types of investing. This is why supporters sometimes are professional investors or angel investors. And typical use cases are early stage, sometimes innovative companies, rather than music, movies, or non-profit projects with social impact.

Equity Crowdfunding: Example

The above figure is an example of equity crowdfunding. The share capital is $1 million, which means Alice, Bob, and Charlie will each have 1% of the share capital. They have invested because they think this café might be profitable.

Crowdlending

In crowdlending, contributors (supporters) receive pre-defined financial rewards (interest) in return for their contribution. Essentially, for contributors, this is a fixed-income investment. The contributors become debtholders. Usually, contributors are mainly motivated by this potential financial reward. A relatively small portion of supporters' motivation might be to help founders or a company to succeed. Borrowers in crowdlending are typically individuals or small businesses.

Crowdlending receives some criticism for providing no diversification. One of the key rules of investing (including lending) is to diversify. This is why lack of diversification is one of the major weaknesses of the crowdlending model. Because in crowdlending model, typically, one contributor lends to one borrower or a few borrowers.

Donations

In donation-based crowdfunding, contributors donate money to help charitable causes. Contributors do not expect anything in return. In this type of crowdfunding, generally, only non-profit organizations and projects are supported. Usually, the use cases are projects with social impact: healthcare, community development, and so on.

Litigation

Litigation crowdfunding is a form of crowdfunding where individuals can financially support legal cases. In exchange, supporters receive a potential share of the monetary outcome. Essentially, they buy a stake in a claim. This approach adds one more way of funding legal battles and gives supporters the opportunity to invest and at the same time, restore justice, in their perspective.

ICO

An ICO (Initial Coin Offering) is a relatively modern fundraising mechanism, where new cryptocurrency projects sell their underlying tokens to the public. Sometimes, this sale is done in exchange for established cryptocurrencies, for example, Bitcoin or Ether. Essentially, it is a type of crowdfunding specific to the blockchain and cryptocurrency world. With this type of crowdfunding, supporters (early investors) are provided with tokens that imply potential future gains.

How This is Changing the Industry

Crowdfunding in a non-digital form has existed for centuries. However, the advent of modern technology, particularly the Internet and online platforms, has magnified its reach and efficiency. Today, technology allows borrowers, founders, innovators, and creators to:

- get the attention of many potential investors using an online platform
- arrange quickly remote legally binding agreements between all parties
- move funds instantly.

Crowdfunding changes the world of finance by bringing in one more way to secure funding. This method especially benefits projects that resonate emotionally, visually, or intuitively with potential backers. Projects that offer a tangible social impact or present a compelling idea often get significant attention and support.

Potential Risks and Challenges

For all types of crowdfunding, besides donations, supporters expect to receive something in return for their funds. This is especially so for equity crowdfunding and crowdlending (as opposed to reward crowdfunding). Usually, in these projects, there is an alternative for those who seek investments. This alternative is to get funds from professional investors (banks, investment companies, etc.). If the founders are trying to crowdfund, this often means they were not able to receive investments from professional investors, which often means that there was a reason why professional investors did not invest.

Investing is a difficult profession. Investment is a full-time job. Professional investors usually are better at assessing project risks. This might mean adverse selection: a lot of projects and individuals try to crowdfund, because they have gotten "no" from professional investors and financial companies.

Imagine that you are not a doctor, but you must cure a person for some reason. Would you be concerned if professional doctors have already given up on him?

Investing in many countries is a very regulated area. This sometimes means, for example, that only investors who meet certain requirements can invest in equity if the company is not public yet. This is why equity crowdfunding in many countries is heavily regulated because of the risks of fraud and manipulation.

Often, there is a high probability of the company failing and investors getting zero returns. Because of the project's early stage, there are few predictors of success yet; for example, there is usually no history of previous earnings. Also, there is often a lack of reliable information, like audited financial statements. Possible fraudulent crowdfunding is one of the reasons why investors need protection. This is why one of the challenges for equity crowdfunding development is stringent regulation.

Quiz

QUESTION 1.

I have contributed 100 dollars to a startup that promises to produce a revolutionary, very convenient backpack. In return, this startup promised to send me a backpack when it was ready. I am not getting any shares in the company. Which model is this?

A. Reward crowdfunding.
B. Equity crowdfunding.
C. Crowdlending.

QUESTION 2.

I have contributed 100 dollars to a startup that promises to produce a revolutionary, very convenient backpack. In return, I have got 0.01% of the company's shares. Which model is this?

A. Reward crowdfunding.
B. Equity crowdfunding.
C. Crowdlending.

QUESTION 3.

I have contributed 100 dollars to a startup that promises to produce a revolutionary, very convenient backpack. In return, I will get 105 dollars in one year. Which model is this?

A. Reward crowdfunding.
B. Equity crowdfunding.
C. Crowdlending.

QUESTION 4.

What is equity crowdfunding?

A. Equity crowdfunding, also known as crowdinvesting, is a method of raising funds by offering contributors (backers) rewards or perks.
B. Equity crowdfunding, also known as crowdinvesting, is a method of raising funds by offering contributors (backers) stakes (shares) in the company.
C. Equity crowdfunding, also known as crowdinvesting, is a method of raising loans from a relatively large number of individual contributors.

QUESTION 5.

Why is equity crowdfunding quite regulated in many countries?

A. One of the key reasons is investor protection. Companies that get equity crowdfunded are often at the very early stages, or do not even exist yet. This means that often, there is a high probability of failure of the company and investors getting zero returns. Possible fraudulent crowdfunding is another reason why investors need protection.
B. One of the key reasons is equity crowdfunding is usually applicable only to the companies that operate in heavily regulated industries, such as energy and utilities or aviation.
C. Both A and B are correct.

Companies and Platforms to Follow

- Kickstarter (https://www.kickstarter.com/) is a US-based reward crowdfunding platform, one of the largest globally.
- StartEngine (https://www.startengine.com/) is one of the largest equity crowdfunding platforms in the US.

Answers to Quiz

1. **Answer: A.** Reward crowdfunding. I am not getting any shares in the company, and I am not getting my money back. This is reward crowdfunding.
2. **Answer: B.** Equity crowdfunding (also known as equity crowdfunding). I am getting shares in the company. This is equity crowdfunding.
3. **Answer: C.** Crowdlending. I am not getting any shares in the company. I am getting my money back with interest.
4. **Answer: B.** Equity crowdfunding, also known as crowdinvesting, is a method of raising funds by offering contributors (backers) stakes (shares) in the company.
5. **Answer: A.** Statement B is not correct. Crowdfunding is not usually applicable only to the companies that operate in heavily regulated industries.

CHAPTER 8

Insurtech

"Honey, what scares me – this new insurance company knows me even better than your mother does!"

This chapter explains what insurtech is and what its key areas are. The chapter offers the classification of insurtech and explains how insurtech disrupts the traditional insurance world. It covers what drives insurtech and the potential challenges it faces.

In this chapter

What Insurtech Is

Insurtech is a set of modern technologies and business models based on these technologies that disrupt and transform the insurance market. Insurtech is not a specific new insurance product or new business model. Insurtech is an umbrella term. Insurtech is driven by a variety of new technologies, including big data, advanced analytics, AI (Artificial Intelligence), telematics, and the Internet of Things (IoT).

The word "insurtech" is a combination of two words: "insurance" and "technology." Insurtech is about the use of technological innovations for insurance. Insurtech is the insurance part of fintech.

Example

Imagine you own a car, and you want to buy third-party liability insurance. One of the insurance companies offered you the following. You can buy insurance, and at the same time, the insurance company will install a gadget into your car. This gadget will send some information about your driving in real-time. Based on this information, you can get the price you are paying reduced if you demonstrate that you drive responsibly. This is an example of insurtech, because the insurance company leverages modern technology, which substantially changes the way this company operates.

Insurtech: Basics

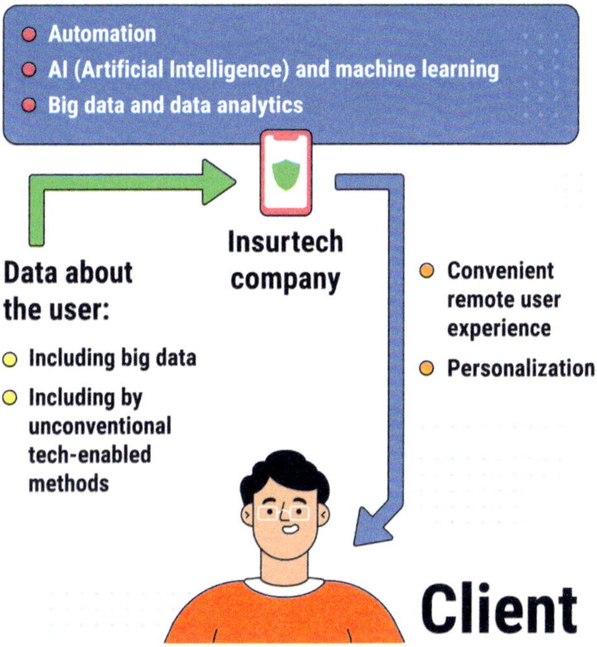

Typically, an insurtech company incorporates some of the following key features. The company employs process automation extensively: AI as well as big data and data analytics. The company collects user data through unconventional, tech-enabled methods like the Internet of Things (IoT) and telematics. The focus is on delivering a convenient, remote user experience that is highly personalized.

Key Areas of Insurtech

Insurtech is a set of modern technologies and business models based on these technologies. These are the key areas (or “types”) of insurtech:

- A focus on remote services with no (or almost no) brick-and-mortar branches. We can call these companies "neo insurance companies," similar to neobanks.
- More advanced data analysis and, as a result, better risk modeling and more attractive pricing.
- Hyper-personalization (often real-time) with flexible tariffs and policies.
- Automation and digitalization of all areas and processes. One of the key examples of this area is the efficient processing of claims: chatbots 24/7, automated processing of documents, automated fraud detection, etc.
- Using sensors, the Internet of Things (IoT), and drones.
- New means of assessment and usage of new types of data. One of the key examples of this area is the analysis of everything that happens on your smartphone.
- Insurance-as-a-service (IaaS) and embedded insurance.

Many (and maybe most) insurtech companies and insurtech services of traditional insurance companies leverage more than one model listed above.

Three Pillars of Insurtech

No legacy (software, processes, people)

No (or almost no) brick and mortar branches

Intelligent services based on modern technologies

Like neobanks, it is important for a modern insurance company to have no legacy of software, business processes, personnel, and so on. The three pillars of the insurtech company are: no legacy, focus on remote service, and intelligent services based on modern technologies.

What Exactly Insurtech is Changing

What exactly is insurtech changing, and why is it disruptive? There are several key areas that are being transformed:

- Costs are down with the help of advanced data analytics methods.
- Costs are down via overall automation and, hence, overall efficiency.

- Products and services become hyper-personalized with the help of advanced data analytics methods.
- User experience gets more convenient. An example is an advanced chatbot in the app 24/7 to process claims and so on.
- New user experiences are added. An example is a functionality for insurance companies to get auto-notification in the case of a car accident via telematics.
- Insurance gets embedded into other user experiences and non-financial products.

Sensors, Telematics, and the Internet of Things

Telematics and the Internet of Things (IoT) are two important concepts for insurtech. These two technologies are significantly changing how insurance companies operate, how they gather information about a user, and what products and services they offer.

Sensors play an important role in many insurtech models by providing real-time data. This data can be used to assess risks and predict potential incidents. With integrated sensors, insurtech companies can monitor various parameters, such as driving habits in car insurance or home conditions in property insurance.

Telematics and the Internet of Things allow insurtech companies to receive detailed, real-time insights into insured assets and behaviors. This real-time data allows companies to offer new user experiences, offer personalized premiums, prevent losses with alerts, and better assess claims.

Getting Information

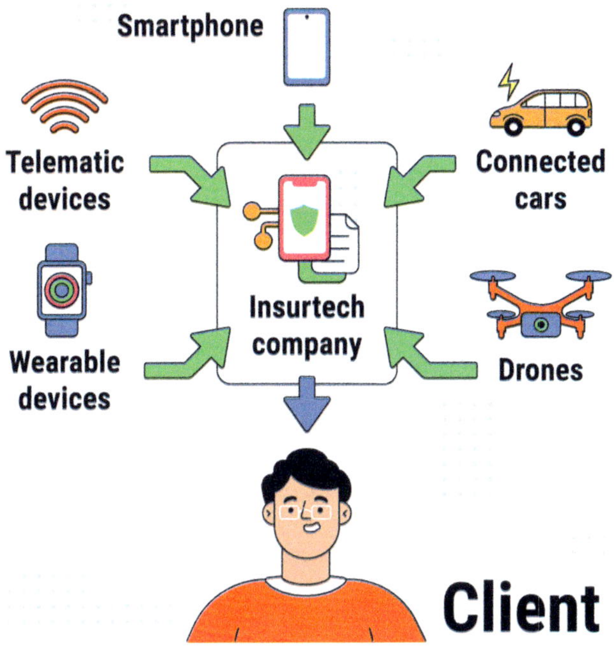

One of the important areas of insurtech is leveraging modern ways of getting data and new types of data to analyze customers, prospective customers, and insured assets. Many insurtech companies gather information by using modern technology: wearable devices, telematic devices, smartphones, connected cars, drones, and so on.

Insurance-as-a-Service

Similar to the popular concept of banking-as-a-service (BaaS), insurance-as-a-service (IaaS) is a model of financial services in which a non-insurance company outsources insurance services for its clients to a third party. This "third party" is the provider of insurance-as-a-service.

Embedded Insurance

One of the key things that transforms customer experience in the world of insurance is customers' ability to buy the insurance policy automatically. Imagine, for example, you are buying a car. You can spend a lot of time researching which insurance to buy. And then again, a lot of time on paperwork. Instead, if your auto dealer includes insurance in the deal, you can have an insurance policy automatically. Ideally, you are required to do a couple of additional mouse clicks in your user journey. These clicks might allow you to see different insurance options and providers, compare them, choose which one is the right option for you, and confirm the service.

Embedded Insurance: Example

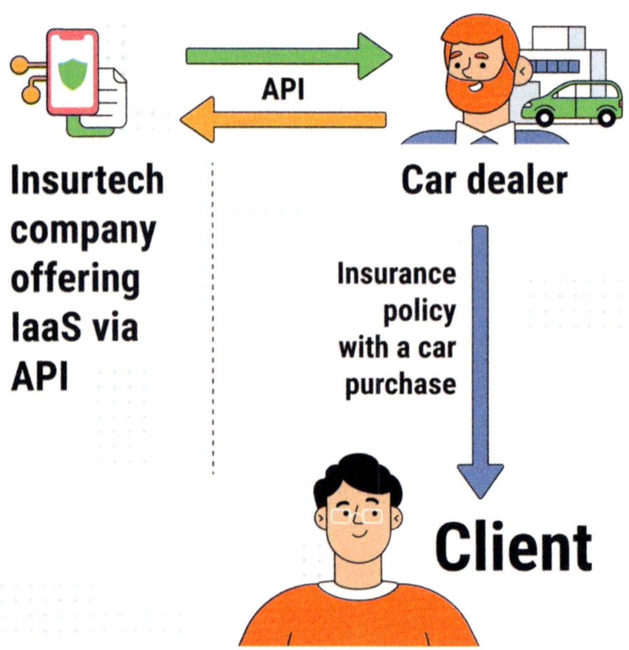

The above figure is an example of embedded insurance. You are buying a car and insurance is embedded in your deal.

API

In the context of insurtech, a very important concept is the API (Application Programming Interface). API allows, in practice, the portability of information. An API is a set of rules, protocols, and standards that allows different software applications to communicate with each other. API allows one organization to get customers' information from another organization in real-time. API provides predefined programming functions and methods, enabling software developers to access and retrieve specific data.

What Drives Insurtech

The development of insurtech is driven mainly through the rapid development of the following areas of technology: advanced data analytics, big data, AI (Artificial Intelligence), sensors, Internet of Things (IoT), and telematics. Aside from these technologies, of course, Internet connectivity and the rapid adoption of smartphones also drive insurtech. All these areas of technology create opportunities to offer substantially different services in a very conservative industry.

How This is Changing the Insurance Industry

Insurance is a very conservative industry. For centuries, the insurance market was notorious for its entry barriers – reputation, economies of scale, capital requirements, etc. And now is the time when technology can change the existing insurance landscape and disrupt the insurance market. Insurtech enables new products, cheaper and better user experiences, more flexible insurance, and so on.

As insurtech reshapes the insurance landscape, it presents significant opportunities for both new startups entering the market and established companies ready to reinvent their approach. This transformation is particularly beneficial for new startups entering the market. Additionally, insurtech creates new opportunities for some suppliers: for example, producers of telematic devices. Also, there are opportunities for software platforms that enable insurance companies to deploy innovative products and services quickly – for example, embed insurance into non-insurance user experiences.

Potential Risks and Challenges

Insurtech companies' history is much shorter than the history of traditional companies. These young companies are yet to build brands and reputations, which are very important in the world of finance. Many customers trust traditional insurance companies more. Young companies' lack of trust and reputation is a hurdle in their development. Many potential customers have seen insurtech companies as early-stage startups, most of which will not survive. So, they are definitely not to be trusted. This perception is changing steadily as many insurtech companies are now stronger, more dynamic, and established – yet young – companies rather than startups.

Another challenge insurtech is facing is regulatory hurdles. Traditionally, insurance has been quite a regulated industry. It is important for governments to make sure insurance companies are able and willing to meet their obligations. Sometimes, innovation happens much faster than slow governments can react. But when they react, they are creating some requirements that might be difficult to comply with.

In insurance, historical data and actuarial mathematics are fundamental to assessing risks and ensuring long-term solvency. New insurtech companies lack a substantial track record to validate their risk models. This is why insurtech companies sometimes have less trust from potential customers and regulators than established companies.

Some insurtech companies aim to gather a diverse range of data from multiple sources about their customers and potential customers. These companies need this data for risk assessment and customer profiling. Regulators impose a lot of limitations on the types of information that can be used. Two major reasons are: data privacy concerns and fairness issues. This regulatory pressure creates additional hurdles for insurtech.

Quiz

QUESTION 1.

What is insurtech?

A. A type of insurance policy for IT (Information Technology) companies.
B. Insurtech is a set of modern technologies and business models based on these technologies, disrupting and transforming the insurance market.
C. Modern insurance products enabled by telematics.

QUESTION 2.

What are the drivers of insurtech?

A. A set of modern technologies – advanced analytics, telematics, the Internet of Things (IoT), and so on.
B. Development of social media platforms.
C. Advancements in AI (Artificial Intelligence).

QUESTION 3.

What is the impact of insurtech on the financial markets and customers?

A. Improvements in customer experience.
B. Enhancing the efficiency of insurance operations.
C. Both A and B are correct answers.

QUESTION 4.

What are the key opportunities for the new companies in the area of insurtech?

A. New companies can disrupt the market and win the competition by offering insurance with substantially lower prices, personalization, and better user experience.
B. New companies can disrupt the market and win the competition by offering non-insurance products in addition to insurance products.
C. New companies can disrupt the market and win the competition by offering insurance products to those customers who are not able to get insurance products from traditional insurance companies.

QUESTION 5.

What are the key challenges of insurtech companies in their development aside from competition from traditional insurance companies?

A. Gaining customers' trust and building brand recognition.
B. Advancements in the Internet of Things (IoT) and telematics.
C. Both A and B.

Companies to Follow

- Cuvva (https://www.cuvva.com/) is a UK-based insurtech company that aims to transform the area of car insurance. Cuvva disrupts the market by introducing flexible and affordable insurance plans.
- Lemonade (https://www.lemonade.com) is a US-based insurtech company. Lemonade offers several types of insurance policies and is most famous for its disruption in property insurance. It uses modern technology to transform how an insurance company works, such as efficient chatbots to process claims. Lemonade aims to make all parts of the insurance process quick and efficient.
- Oscar Health (https://www.hioscar.com/) is a US-based insurtech company that offers medical insurance. Oscar Health transforms insurance by leveraging technology, including data analytics, to offer a personalized and easy health insurance user experience.

Answers to Quiz

1. **Answer: B.** Answer C is not correct because modern insurance products enabled by telematics are only a subset of insurtech.

2. **Answer: A.** Development of social media platforms is rather not one of the key drivers of insurtech. Advancements in AI (Artificial Intelligence) are only one of the technological trends that drive insurtech.

3. **Answer: C.** Both improvements in customer experience and enhanced efficiency of insurance operations are two outcomes of the development of insurtech.

4. **Answer: A.** New companies might offer non-insurance products to those customers who are not able to get insurance products from traditional insurance companies. But, the key opportunities in the insurtech lie in the tech-enabled offerings with substantially lower prices, personalization, and better user experience.

5. **Answer: A.** Advancements in the Internet of Things (IoT) and telematics are not key challenges. Rather, they are some of the technological trends that drive the development of insurtech. The correct answer is A.

CHAPTER 9

Robo-Advising

"Honey, remember that guy in expensive suit who has been losing money for us? Now we can manage ourselves!"

This chapter explains what a robo-advisor and robo-advising are. It also explains how robo-advisors help build, adjust, and rebalance an investment portfolio. The chapter covers how robo-advisors change the world of financial services and what drives the development of robo-advisors. Additionally, it discusses the opportunities that the robo-advisor concept brings and the key challenges faced in the advancement of robo-advisory.

In this chapter

What a Robo-Advisor Is

A robo-advisor is an automated IT-enabled investment advisory and money management tool. Robo-advisors help build, adjust, and rebalance an investment portfolio. Robo-advisors also help in the investment portfolio's loss harvesting and taxation optimization. A robo-advisor has nothing to do with robots. It is a type of software product.

Example

Let's say you would like to invest your savings. Instead of hiring a traditional asset management advisor (a human), you can just open a website. Instead of picking the assets for your portfolio yourself, you can delegate that to a robo-advisor. The robo-advisor creates a personalized portfolio for you.

Robo-Advisor: Basics

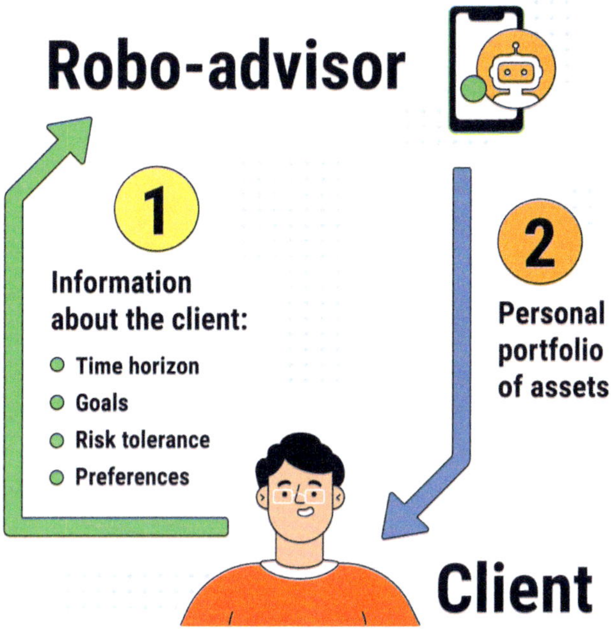

A robo-advisor collects information about the customer. This information helps the robo-advisor to formulate customers' time horizon, goals, risk tolerance (also known as risk appetite), and preferences. Based on that, the robo-advisor builds a tailored portfolio of assets for this customer.

How a Robo-Advisor Works

Robo-advisory means tailored service. So, first of all, a robo-advisor gathers some inputs about the customer. These inputs are customers' time horizon, goals, risk tolerance, and preferences.

For example:

- Time horizon. You are planning to buy a house in five years and retire in 10 years. These two major events will define your time horizon.

- Goals. You are planning to accumulate 200 thousand dollars for buying a house, and you would like to have an annual income of 50 thousand dollars after retirement. These are your goals.
- Risk tolerance. Your risk tolerance is moderate, you already have some assets (aside from the investment portfolio you are about to create) and a pension.
- Preferences. You would like to invest at least 10% of your assets in companies that are involved in green renewable energy production.

The robo-advisor defines your individual investment strategy and asset allocation based on these inputs. Next, the robo-advisor creates a personalized portfolio that is optimal for you. After that, the robo-advisor constantly monitors this portfolio and rebalances the portfolio if and when needed.

Sometimes, people believe that a human advisor knows or must know some magical secrets, for example, which shares will rise in value tomorrow. In reality, an advisor's job is often about taking several simple steps. Even though sometimes advisors try hard to prove otherwise and wear expensive suits. These steps can be done by software. For example, if you are young, investment theory says your share of equity (versus bonds) should be higher. There is an optimal share of equity (given other inputs). So, an advisor defines the optimal proportion of equity (versus bonds and other types of assets) for a given age. This is one parameter. There are many parameters, but the algorithm can describe all of them. In robo-advisory, this algorithm is coded into the robo-advisory software.

The Stages of the Investment Process

These are the stages of the investment process – stages of what an investment advisor does:

- getting information about the client
- setting goals
- assessing risk tolerance

- creating an individual investment strategy
- asset allocation and security selection
- building a portfolio – execution
- monitoring and rebalancing
- optimizing taxation, including through loss harvesting
- reporting (tax declaration and so on)
- performance monitoring, review, and adjustments.

These stages should be periodically repeated. Any major changes in the client's situation and becoming older means information about the client should be updated. Then, the goals and the risk tolerance are reassessed. The individual investment strategy is updated, and so on.

Let's see how robo-advisory transforms these stages into a convenient, remote, cost-effective digital experience.

Automated questionnaires, data analysis, and quantitative models help gather information about the client and define their goals and risk tolerance. This digital experience is often significantly more convenient for clients and more cost-effective. Then, the robo-advisor's algorithms define an individual customized investment strategy, optimal asset allocation, and security selection. Then, the robo-advisors execute trades automatically, often faster and with lower costs than human advisors.

Robo-advisors continuously monitor portfolios and automatically rebalance them to maintain target allocations. This is one of the advantages of robo-advisors because, for human advisors, continuous monitoring is nearly impossible.

Robo-advisors use algorithms to optimize tax efficiency, including tax-loss harvesting, within client portfolios. This stage often includes complex, tedious calculations, which are the areas where algorithms beat humans by a wide margin. Finally, robo-advisors quickly and cost-effectively generate necessary reports automatically.

Personalized Portfolio

Based on your information, a robo-advisor defines your individual investment strategy and optimal asset allocation. Then, the robo-advisor creates a personalized portfolio that is optimal for you. The robo-advisor constantly monitors and rebalances this portfolio.

Types of Robo-Advisors

There are many ways in which robo-advisors can be classified. First, there are two types of companies:

- Standalone robo-advisory companies. These are oftentimes relatively new, dynamically growing companies focused on technology.

- A robo-advisory product inside a money management company. This is a product of a traditional company built around traditional finance.

Secondly, two common types of robo-advisors are:

- Robo-advisors offering only advice. The output of this advisor is recommendations regarding your optimal portfolio.
- Full cycle of money management (or almost full cycle): advice and execution (including brokerage).

Another way to classify robo-advisors is by level of human intervention:

- Pure robo-advisory
- Significant human intervention: customers' ability to get live advice
- Anything in between: various combinations offering a blend of automation and human interaction.

The Right Mix of Automation and Human Help

The convergence of robo-advisors with traditional financial tools has led to a diverse array of products, offering a blend of automation and human interaction. Many users value the efficiency and precision of modern technology but also find reassurance in having access to personalized support and guidance from live advisors. Thus, numerous investment management companies today are trying to strike the right balance between automation and the human touch.

Hyper-Personalization

Robo-advisory can be considered as hyper-personalization in the world of money management. Hyper-personalization of financial services refers to the deep customization of financial services to meet individual or prospective customers' specific goals, situations, and preferences. This is enabled by modern advanced technology, including big data, advanced data analytics, and machine learning, that allows financial institutions to (1) gather a lot of near real-time data, including big data, about a customer, (2) analyze this data, and (3) quickly offer and deliver the service to meet specific needs and preferences.

Affordable, Yet Personalized

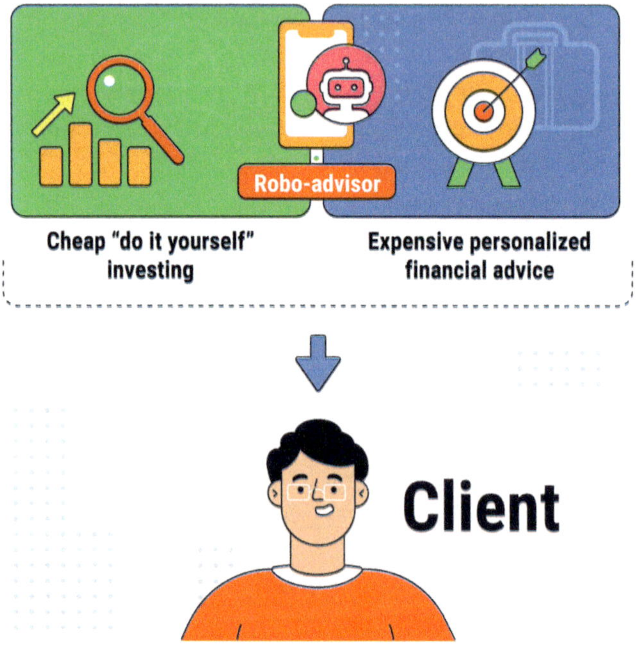

Robo-advisory democratizes investment management by creating affordable yet hyper-personalized service. Robo-advising makes optimal, proficient investing accessible.

What Drives Robo-Advising

In some fields, algorithms can do the same job as humans, often better and cheaper. Money management is one of the activities that can be algorithmized and performed by software. Paraphrasing a famous quote (Marc Andreessen: "…software is eating the world"): software is eating money management.

Additionally, a driving force behind the development of robo-advisors, similar to the development in many other areas of fintech, is the widespread and affordable access to the Internet and smartphones. Today, smartphones (and computers) are affordable for almost everyone, and Internet connectivity is available almost everywhere around the world. These facts have facilitated the digitalization of many areas of our lives, including money management.

How Robo-Advising is Changing the Industry

Robo-advising revolutionizes the money management industry and democratizes professional investment management advice – making it accessible for someone who is not able to pay a hefty amount for it. Software replaces the traditional human-intensive business model. Robo-advising makes optimal, proficient investing accessible to virtually everyone.

This disruption creates significant opportunities for new players. They are more focused on technology than traditional players and can offer a better user experience with lower costs. Thus, they can compete successfully with traditional companies, attracting clients, particularly younger ones. These clients are either switching from traditional money management companies or starting to use money management services for the first time in their lives.

For traditional companies, robo-advising brings opportunities as well: efficiency, cost reduction, and better user experience. Traditional companies have their own advantages in competition with startups: reputation, an existing clientele, and live consultants, who can be handy in the hybrid model.

Robo-advising offers numerous job opportunities for IT (Information Technology) professionals: software developers, designers, user experience specialists, testers, and so on. While robo-advising disrupts the financial advisor profession, it creates more highly desired white-collar positions in the IT domain.

Potential Risks and Challenges

Aside from the typical challenges many fintech players face, such as regulatory compliance, robo-advisory has one particular challenge. Imagine that your human financial advisor makes a mistake. For example, your asset allocation is sub-optimal. It's a problem for you, but only for you. If a robo-advisor makes a mistake, it is very likely that the mistake will be scaled and replicated across multiple portfolios. For robo-advisory, ensuring that the algorithms of software are accurate and reliable is critical to providing sound investment advice.

Another challenge that arises is the apprehension users feel towards self-service in such a crucial aspect of their lives. The idea of not sharing responsibility with another human that you can see and speak to can be daunting. Many worry about the possibility of making a mistake. This fear can be a significant barrier to adopting robo-advisors.

Quiz

QUESTION 1.

What is a robo-advisor?

A. Robo-advisor is a machine that offers advice on investment topics in a manner similar to a human.
B. Robo-advisor is an automated, IT-enabled investment advisory and money management tool.
C. Robo-advisor is an automated, IT-enabled advisory on a wide range of topics in finance, such as which credit card to choose, how to refinance your mortgage, and so on.

QUESTION 2.

What are some of the key differences between robo-advisors and traditional money managers?

A. Algorithms exclude the emotional component from their decision-making process. This is one of the reasons the robo-advising approach is more disciplined and yields, on average, better results.
B. Traditional money managers might have a subjective view of the methodology of investments and optimal asset allocation. As a result of this subjective opinion, investors' results might deviate significantly from the optimal outcome.
C. Both A and B are correct.

QUESTION 3.

How are robo-advisors disrupting financial markets?

A. They offer more affordable personalized advice, leading many to switch.
B. The user experience is enhanced – it's fully remote, more intuitive, and provides superior user interfaces that many find easier to understand.
C. Both A and B are correct.

QUESTION 4.

What are the opportunities for companies and startups that the concept of robo-advisory brings?

A. For existing asset management companies: cost reductions by increasing efficiency and better user experience, thus attracting new customers and giving better results for existing customers.
B. For new players: an opportunity to offer a product more competitive compared to the product offered by many traditional asset management companies.
C. Both A and B are correct.

QUESTION 5.

What is one of the key challenges and problems in the advancement of robo-advisors?

A. Regulatory pressure, as regulators in many countries are very opposed to the concept of robo-advising.
B. The potential risk of a mistake in the algorithm leading to inaccuracies, because algorithms might not always be accurate and reliable.
C. Higher costs for users as opposed to traditional tools and services.

Companies and Products to Follow

- Betterment (https://www.betterment.com) is a US-based robo-advisory company. It is one of the first and most prominent robo-advisors in the world. Betterment was founded in 2008.
- Wealthfront (https://www.wealthfront.com) is a US-based robo-advisory company. It is one of the first and most prominent robo-advisory companies. It was founded in 2008.
- Vanguard Personal Advisor Services (https://investor.vanguard.com/) is a robo-advisory product of one of the leading traditional asset management companies, Vanguard. This product combines pure robo-advisory with traditional human help. This product has been built around the traditional financial products.

Answers to Quiz

1. **Answer: B.** Choice A is not correct, as a robo-advisor is a software product, not a machine. Choice C is not correct because, typically, a robo-advisor is understood to be a product whose scope is limited to investments: it does not cover all areas of finance.

2. **Answer: C.** Both A and B accurately depict some of the key differences between robo-advisors and traditional money managers.

3. **Answer: C.** Both A and B accurately depict the benefits of robo-advisors, showcasing how they are revolutionizing the financial markets.

4. **Answer: C.** Both A and B correctly describe the concept that robo-advisory brings.

5. **Answer: B.** Choice A is not entirely correct, as regulatory pressure is rather not a major challenge for robo-advisors. Choice C is not correct because robo-advisors are usually able to offer lower fees than traditional companies.

Please email me at sergey@tsabolov.com to let me know if you liked this book. This is invaluable to me – to hear from my readers!

Please email me what you did not like and what you would change or add. I would love to hear your opinion. I want to base the next editions' corrections and updates on the readers' feedback.

Thank you very much! I appreciate your help!

Sergey Tsabolov

Printed in Great Britain
by Amazon

54410058R00109